BLACK
SABBATH

Printed in the UK by MPG Books, Bodmin

Published by Sanctuary Publishing Limited, Sanctuary House,
45-53 Sinclair Road, London W14 0NS, United Kingdom

www.sanctuarypublishing.com

ISBN: 1-86074-458-3

Steven Rosen

BLACK SABBATH

with Special Guest Foreword by

Ozzy Osbourne

Sanctuary

Acknowledgements

To the people who made this book possible by giving me complete Sanctuary, I thank: Penny Braybrooke, Michelle Knight, Chris Bradford and Dan Froude. A huge thanks to Alan Heal for helping me get the words right, and a monstrous and rabid thanks to Jeff Hudson for putting out a night light for a wandering journalist.

To my mom, who instilled in me the love of language, and to my dad, who showed me love of music; my younger brother, Mick ("not Nick"), who cared enough to yell at me; and to my sister-in-law for caring enough to love my brother. All the believers: Beverly, Jack Holtzclaw, Jay Lawson, Aeron Ward, Brian (the runner), Cee, Barry Goldberg, Peter Kelsey, Buddy Brundo, Charlene Skeffington, Ronnie Ciago, Keith Lynch, Paul Ill, Stephan Ferrera-Grand, Mike Slarve, Jim Warino, Lisa Gladfelter, Mark "Gopher" Smith, Jimmy and Joanne Waldo, Donnie Jones, Jackie, Julia S Roberts, David Konow, Chris "K" Kinderman, Mr Swanson (my eighth-grade English teacher, who told me to write), Mrs Carpenter (my tenth-grade journalism teacher, who taught me more than she realised), Rhonda Saenz, Neal Zlozower. And, to those of you I've forgotten, my apologies. I'll get you next time.

Dedicated thanks to the players who found time to be interrogated: Vinnie and Carmine Appice, Ernie C, Joe Holmes, Zakk Wylde, Brad Gillis, Jake E Lee, Steve Vai, Glenn Hughes and Neil Murray.

Especial nods to the Sab Four themselves for opening their heads and hearts in order to bring true life to the project. One individual in particular gave freely of his knowledge and insight. He didn't want me to make a big to-do about this, so I won't. You know who you are, and I'll be forever grateful.

Lastly, and most importantly, all you Saboteurs who loved this band unconditionally and thus established them as true pioneers.

Every interview in this book was personally conducted by this author during a period spanning more than 20 years. I did utilise research materials, simply for background filler, but the essential text was culled from conversations transpiring over the past couple of decades.

Steven Rosen
West Hollywood, California
October 2001

Contents

'God Sprinkled Stardust'

by Bill Ward

Dear reader, my name is Bill Ward and this poem is for you and Ozzy and Tony and Geezer, whom I will always support and love.

God sprinkled stardust over the 100-year-old houses,
When gaslights still brought puddles of street moons
    to dance in
From light to dark, from dark to light
Dearest, strangled Aston,
Determined Aston.

In rage and forgiving all in one
Born and raised four sons
Who caressed and held each other,
Cried, kicked, bated and loved.

Never have I seen such energy
Thousands have been influenced,
Millions have watched and listened.
What pain, what love, each one
Needing the other. Grand days.

What was the greatest
Gig? it's been asked. I have said,
When there was no more strength,
When tiredness dominated
And loneliness seeped
Into the very arms, lungs
And fingers, urging,
Get thee from here.

Inevitably, showtime came and
The energy, the phenomenon
Of one of the greatest
Rock bands in history soared
And broke loose from its
Earthly, selfish bondage
And rocked and rocked and rocked and rocked.

With love,
Bill.

Foreword

by Ozzy Osbourne

 After speaking with Steven for a few minutes today, I remembered the first time we met, back on 12 February 1974, when Sabbath was in St Louis. Steven reminded me that we destroyed his hotel room – we set a couch on fire, tore pictures from the walls, ripped the television from its base and pushed it into the hallway and sprayed the entire room and everyone in it with a fire extinguisher. I seem to remember some girl named Stormy Monday, and somewhere along the way I was handcuffed and arrested. It's hard to remember exactly what happened, but Steven said it was a fun night. That was 27 years ago.

Then I started getting loads of emails in the Ozzy chatroom and they were saying it would be cool if Ozzy got back together with Black Sabbath. I did 'The Wizard' for the first time in 30 years at the Ozzfest and it was, like, "Oh, my fucking God!" Somebody came up to me after I played it and said, "Now we know you weren't playing the harmonica." I said, "I fucking was!" If the kids had written that the best thing I ever did was splitting from Sabbath and "We love you more now," I never would have gone back with the band, but I gave people what they wanted. I didn't force Sabbath on them.

At the beginning of 2001, we all got together in this place we used to use years ago in Wales called the Rockfield Studio. We had a few song ideas, but what might materialise from that I really didn't know. We played one of those songs at the Ozzfest called 'Scary Dreams'. To be honest, I thought at a certain point in the song that it needed to pick up and rock a bit more.

I got my ass beat up for a lot of years because they fired me and I said, "Fuck you, I'll never play with you again." Tony, in the old days, would intimidate the fucking shit out of me. He was, like, a bad dude, sometimes, so I was pleasantly surprised. He'd been beaten down to the ground with Black Sabbath and we're really good friends now. If nothing ever happens again, we played together, we all got a fair shake and we became friends again.

It wasn't the same, though. How could it be? All I can say is that I buried the hatchet, I made friends with the people I thought I'd never speak to again for the rest of my life and I'll never say never again.

The thing is, there's Ozzy in a lot of people – everybody would like to be Ozzy for an hour – and back in 1974 Steven had a chance to be Ozzy for an hour when we burned down his hotel room. I haven't read the book, but I know that he never asked me questions like, "What did the bat taste like?" So I told him I'd be happy to write this intro. And I hope you, the reader, is happy reading it.

Ozzy Osbourne

Author's Insight

I first met them in 1974 during the North American leg of their Sabbath Bloody Sabbath tour and, like many of you, I already had a pretty well-defined image of what to expect. By that time, they already had four or five years in developing their musical profile, one based on the dark and nether-shadowed side of things. The logical side of my brain knew that this character transformation was simply a ploy, a stunt they pulled merely to sell records and concert tickets, and that they no more believed in the Devil or black magic than did any normal God-fearing, church-going, moral-abiding album buyer.

But a tiny voice inside me whispered ever so softly, "What if? What if?" and set up a mini-IV drip and hooked it to the opposite side of my brain, the illogical half harbouring doubts and trepidation and superstition. Coming from Hollywood, where the phantasmagorical crosses over to the physical realm several times a day, there was still a part of me which was…well, not exactly spooked, but rather was suspicious. I was, after all, meeting with Ozzy and his three-man coven, and at the first sign of levitation, de-materialisation or physical transformation, my non-believing soul was on the next plane home.

I land in St Louis, Missouri, where the band has sold out the mammoth Kiel Auditorium and am greeted by a limousine, which whisks me to my hotel. If these guys are Beelzebub believers, they are not ignorant of earthly pleasures. A stretch beats the hell out of riding on the rear of a broomstick. I cruise to the hotel, check in and see a red buzzer light flashing on the phone. A red light? Aren't these signals usually yellow or blue? A blood-red light winks at me like a bloodshot cyclops. I call in for the message and the front desk informs me, "The band wants to meet you now. Come immediately to room 666." I've seen my share of *Exorcist* movies, and even I know that 666 is the sign of the Antichrist. Wait, I'm kidding; it isn't room 666 (and in fact I have no idea what the suite locale was). Kidding, just stirring up the brew. I saunter down to their room, knock softly and am ushered in. All four members are there, and immediately they cease, mid-sacrifice, the lamb they are beheading.

Again, I'm pulling your leg. Many of you want, or are trying, to believe that this group of Englishmen truly indulge in the rituals associated with the fawning over of the fallen angel himself, but nothing could be further from the truth. They were as normal and/or weird as you and me, and in fact it struck me instantly how truly polite, professional and genuinely honest they were.

They introduced themselves – Ozzy Osbourne, Tony Iommi, Geezer Butler and Bill Ward – shook my hand as if they meant it and right away told me that, if there was anything I needed, I should let them know. I was given total access, the golden laminate, interview times, round-the-clock transportation and a general feeling of welcome.

All this is by way of saying that Black Sabbath was, and still are, simply four boys from Aston, England, a suburb of Birmingham, a town chipped and chiselled and face-lifted by the multitude of bombs that rained upon it during the war. Music became a refuge, an umbrella under which they could hide and feel temporarily safe from the horrors swirling about them. The anger and venom and unreality of their music was a natural outgrowth of living amidst air-raid warnings, demolished buildings and the uncertainty of what tomorrow may or may not bring.

In a sense, then, Black Sabbath created sounds born from the bombed-out, lifeless and, at times, hopeless vapours that covered the town of Aston like a suffocating shroud. Someone once said, "If they give you rocks, build a rock garden. If you end up with lemons, stir up a pitcher of lemonade." Survival for these four dreamers meant creating from chaos, and thus the poisons and penetrating malaise which constantly surrounded them became a conduit of construction. They never allowed themselves to become victims, and as you read on it will become apparent just how victorious this band was, on so many levels.

Even when the band attained levels of success and recognition few other ensembles ever tasted, they were still dismissed by anal and near-sighted critics as a heavy metal band dealing in broad strokes and oblivious of the intricacies inherent in "real" music. (The same lame comments were directed at another Birmingham-based band, Led Zeppelin.) So you be the judge. Sabbath was experimenting with synthesisers, acoustic instruments, flutes, live percussion, vocal chorales and many other tragically unhip elements very early in their career, but all anyone ever focused on were Iommi's guitar licks and Ozzy's tattoos.

Black Sabbath emerged during a period in music which any purist or record buyer with even a scintilla of awareness will tell you was the true golden age. They say that smell is the strongest memory trigger, the olfactory sense conjuring up moments of our lives long past gone. A newly-cut lawn, pancakes browning in a mother's kitchen – these simple sensory motivators are capable of whisking you back to a time you felt was all but forgotten. But the Sabs, unfolding their wings during the late '60s and early '70s, were at the perfect place at the perfect time. Bands were autonomous, individualistic, and no two groups sounded alike. And so, while many keyed on nose music as a temporal ladder of what they'd been through, an entire generation marked the passage of years via the auditory canals. What they were listening to was their yardstick.

The first Led Zeppelin album made many of us weak in the knees, caused our hearts to keep time with John Bonham's bass drum and placed in our grey matter like a permanent probe just where we were and what we were doing the first time we heard the brilliance of 'Good Times Bad Times'. How could anybody's foot move so fast? We had no reference by which to judge these sounds, and this became Ground Zero – everything mushroomed from here. On top of that, there was something slightly menacing about the grooves, the almost virgin-like moaning of Robert Plant and the magic produced by Jimmy Page's guitar. We weren't frightened, just fascinated.

And then, who could ignore Jimi Hendrix's *Are You Experienced?* debut, a black/white man who played his guitar upside down and combined cross-cultural elements with the political and mystical. Hendrix, too, flew with the angels, his music bound by nothing we knew here on Earth. But, at the same time, he had a sinister smile, a devilish grin, and were we to meet him on a dark street, we'd probably cross to the other side.

And finally, in 1970, four minstrels from Aston, England, created a sound at once apocryphal and at the same time Edenesque. This self-named first record was the beginning and ending, the start of a style with no pretence – just guitar, bass and drums locking in on a simple three-note phrase, causing the heart to shake, rattle and roll. The title track was a bludgeoning of the senses. There was no subtlety here, just a sort of controlled dementia. No shades of grey, just black and white and ominous, the first beating of the gong trumpeting what would become, for the Sab Four, a career spanning – in various forms – more than two and a half decades.

Let us return to 1974. I spent several days with the band, talking, interviewing and establishing a friendship that would last over 20 years. Since then, I have spent quite a bit of time with them, and they were never less then tremendously affable and good-hearted. Maybe our relationship stems from the fact that, on the evening after their sold-out concert in St Louis, we trashed a hotel room. Did they do this for my benefit? I don't think so. It started harmlessly – someone ripped a picture from the wall, and if you know anything about the attachment of art in hotel rooms, you know that they don't come off easily. So, photo removed and gaping plaster hole now visible, there was no recourse but to remove all of the photos. Then somebody else (the exact perpetrator now escapes me) found a fire extinguisher in the hallway and proceeded to spray everyone and everything in the room. We walked around like zombies from *Night Of The Living Dead* (somehow *apropos*), beside ourselves with laughter. A cigarette was tossed onto a sofa, said couch began to smoulder and this time the fire extinguisher was used for a practical purpose, but not before the settee was completely burned. (This was the only sacrifice that evening.) A television set was extricated from its lodging and, for the next several hours, was given a free ride up and down the elevator.

Nowhere in all this mayhem was there even a flash of pure violence. The band had carried the spirits of 17,000-plus concert-goers for over two hours, and this was the release, the exorcism of hidden energy reserves. No burned flesh, just a smoking sofa; no cryptic chanting, just a roomful of people letting off excess adrenalin reserves. And I was as guilty as any of them. (In the morning, the band paid for all damages.)

The meaning of this parable, if there is one, is that Black Sabbath was a misunderstood group of players who may have been characterised first and foremost as hell-dwellers rather than four musicians of underrated talents and vision. This book will hopefully reveal the musical side of the band, their interaction with each other as players, the lofty and well-deserved place they hold in the rock world, their continuing influence on contemporary idioms and the basic breakdown of each member – their fears, hopes, dreams, demons and beliefs.

What makes the band even more extraordinary is the length of their reach, the far-flung influence they've had on so many other bands. Here, over 25 years after the release of their first record, Sabbath are still making music. (Although guitarist Tony Iommi is the only original member still carrying the banner, rumours are ripe about a reunion of the principals.) In the span of real time, a quarter of a century is nothing, barely a ripple, a mosquito's teardrop, the single flutter of a hummingbird's wing; but in rock 'n' roll time, 300 months is akin to 1,000 ice ages, Methuselah on his 90th birthday, emptying the River Thames drop by drop with a silver spoon. It's an eternity, a forever, a career span only a handful of artists has ever experienced.

In fact, in 1994, an assembly of bands chose their favourite Sabbath dirge and paid homage on an album titled *Nativity In Black: A Tribute To Black Sabbath*. Biohazard, Megadeth, White Zombie, Sepultura and several others sculpted their own versions of the quartet's classics.

Maybe I shouldn't admit this, but now is as good a time as any. When the first Black Sabbath record was spawned, in 1970, I found on first, second and tenth listenings a certain *laissez-faire* attitude. I just didn't care what they were saying. This vocalist, Ozzy Osbourne, bothered me. He scratched my eardrums like cheese on a grater, and Tony Iommi's guitar canvas was muddied in broad strokes, as if he were playing by numbers. Unlike

Zeppelin's original *tour de force* – a blinding and intoxicating collage of blues and reds, the edginess of Picasso mixed with the seminal stroke of Van Gogh – Black Sabbath appeared to be searching for their own particular shade of pale.

But, on the eleventh listen, their threnodies washed over my brain in a Sabbath of revelation and I heard and was touched by the desperation and anger and immediacy of the music. I was looking for something, and what I didn't understand was that, in the whirled order of Sabbath, they find you. The three-note lament of the title track – a building block upon which thrash, smash and gash music has been constructed – seeps into your brainpan like a slow-acting acid and replaces all reasonable and rational fluids with rock 'n' roll jelly. Sabbath music was like a time-release pill – you had to give it minutes, hours, even days to penetrate but, once soaked in, it never left the system.

Such was my reaction to Sabbath music: a wonderful combination of weirdness, super-unnaturalness and genuinely fanciful technique. These four Birmingham boys created a music together. Not black magic – that was all smoke and mirrors and record company media trash; rather, a sound that went beyond guitar, bass, drums and vocals to encompass a fifth member, that invisible yet tactile element created when this quartet performed together. (Drummer Bill Ward will talk about this fifth member within the main body of this book.)

Some years ago, Black Sabbath played in Ventura, California, a beach community about 45 minutes north of Los Angeles. Tony Iommi, the only remaining original member, ran this latest incarnation through a set which included those beasts that would live forever: 'Iron Man', 'Paranoid' and 'War Pigs'. Iommi performed flawlessly, a little flash but with a depth of expression he always managed to coax from his guitar. I had not seen Tony for some time, and backstage, following the show, he greeted me warmly and gripped my hand sincerely. Dressed like midnight, the tall Englishman grinned and, with a little bit of modesty, intoned, "Well, we're still here." Indeed they are.

1 Bombs Over Birmingham

Aston, England, the home town of Ozzy Osbourne, Tony Iommi, Bill Ward and Geezer Butler, was a place both tender and tough, a city buried beneath the explosives of German bombs and a place steeped in a tradition dating back over 500 years. Often referred to as "the queen of the city", this suburb of Birmingham was a community factory-filled and populated by the people working in them. Home values were stressed, but if you didn't belong to a gang, the chances were that you were in store for a daily thrashing.

This was a chimeric place, then, one of light and shadows, where the daylight hours shone upon the faces of the working class and, when the sun went down, the creatures of the night did their stalkings and hauntings.

Bill Ward, born in Aston on 5 May 1948, remembers his birthplace as a community of sharp edges and polished surfaces. It was a strong influence on what he would later become. "It's a very special place. It's where Birmingham really began. It was mainly factory workers, and of course it was badly bombed during the war, 'cause that's where all the factories were. All the ball-bearing factories, all the foundries and beer companies were in Aston, and all the houses were, like, Victorian in setting, because in Victorian times they would build to go with the workers' houses. So Aston was its own little place. It had its own church, which was about 500 years old. It's a place they called Aston Hall, which dates way back into the 16th century. So it's alway's been there. It's always been this little place inside this massive city.

"Railway trains would come in, big steam trains. The people there were very resilient, and there was a certain… There was a lot of pride, coming from Aston. I sensed that they were prideful people. This was not a rich place at all. Most people were just regular factory workers and they got by and they made do. And they took pride in their houses – they would clean the front steps of their houses. They would make sure the brass was shining on the doors. Most of the houses in Aston were at least 200 years old."

So Birmingham's baby brother (sister?) was a pot-pourri of Dickens and decadence, and these two forces ever weighing upon the young and impressionable played a large part in forming the personalities of the foursome ultimately to become the band known as Black Sabbath. Although the town was strafed unmercifully by German ME-110 twin-engined bomber planes, it persevered with a salt-of-the-earth, never-say-die philosophy, creating a fertile and inviting hotbed for the musically adventurous. Perhaps this was the way in which the city emotionally protected itself – rather than cowering in your house and waiting for the next barrage, the next blitzkrieg, you channelled these feelings into something positive, something uplifting. This may account for the surprising number of bands to emerge from the area, making it, like Liverpool and London, an undisputed music Mecca.

Besides Black Sabbath, this Midlands city was home for groups/soloists such as The Move, The Moody Blues, Clem Clempson (during those days a member of The Bakerloo Blues Band and, later, Colosseum and Humble Pie), Traffic, Robert Plant and John Bonham (a close friend of Ward, a relationship these pages will address later) and a handful of lesser-known artists. Not only was there no dearth of bands but there was also a regular circuit of clubs, bars and halls in which they played. Places like Henry's, Mother's Club and the Town Hall were all venues for bands to sharpen their blades, to turn their musically broad strokes into defined and personality-laden applications. "God is in the details," some wise man once invoked, and it was within these halls – some of them surrounded by the detritus produced by madmen in flying machines – that the broad splashes took on a new focus.

2 And On The First Day,
God Created…Polka Tulk?

Aston, then, was a true breeding ground for musicians, providing many venues in which bands might flex their musical muscles. The only major obstacle was in locating the right people to play with. Unbeknown to William Thomas Ward was the fact that, within the area in which he lived, there were three other musicians, each craving and searching desperately for those missing pieces that would ultimately make them whole: John Michael Osbourne, born on 3 December 1948; Anthony Frank Iommi (of Italian ancestry), born on 19 February 1948; and Terence Michael Butler, born on 17 July 1949. These street urchins grew up within spitting distance of each other, and it really didn't take long for them to find each other.

They all attended school, although more as a way of killing time than anything else. All four had been involved in a series of bands – Bill even played "legit" standards in his school orchestra – but it wasn't until Ward and Iommi started an ensemble called Mythology and Ozzy and Geezer teamed up in Rare Breed that the first real Sabbath seeds were planted. Mythology was little more than a blues band, covering standards and generally blending in as just another of the faceless entities to which Birmingham now seemed to be giving regular birth. Bill and Tony, along with singer Chris Smith, travelled north to Carlisle, where they undertook several gigs as The Rest before changing to Mythology.

"This was way back in the '60s, so it's a little hard to remember everything," muses Ward. "Tony [Iommi] was the first person to join the band. The bass player was with Peter And Gordon. I think he was called Neil, but I forget his last name. Anyway, Neil was the bass player and there was another drummer, a guy called Terry who worked with a band called Black Cat Bones. Then Terry left and Tony called me and said, 'Look, come over to Carlisle.' This band were based in Carlisle, northern England. He said, 'Come up here. We've got a nice little thing going on. Just get on a train and come up and we'll put things together.' And the singer who sang in Mythology was a guy called Chris Smith.

"We were doing some real old blues standard type of things. And Chris was from The Method Five, which was one of the bands that I played with, on and off. Another Birmingham band. So Mythology came out of that. And it was actually a very nice band. It was a lot of fun. Carlisle for me was a good time. It was my first real time that I spent away from Birmingham, and we had a big following there. We played all the clubs, all the places one can play in northern England. It was good."

In the meantime, Ozzy and Geezer were trying to breathe life into their own creation, Rare Breed, but after only two gigs, the patient died. The Rest, since morphing into Mythology, had also run their course, and the guitarist and drummer returned to Aston. In need of another singer and bassist, they found an advert in a local music paper which read, "Ozzy Zig, vocalist, requires band. Owns own PA." Tony had attended school with an Ozzy, but he felt certain that this could not be the same individual. Not only did he not get along with this person, but his schoolmate couldn't sing a note.

"So Bill and I went to see him and, a few days later, Ozzy and Geezer came around to my house, looking for a drummer. And so I said, 'Well, I have Bill Ward.' And then we all just got together. There was already another guitar player – a slide-guitar player – and a sax player on the side. Jimmy Phillips was the slide-guitar player. It was a riot. It was just chaos.

"It was blues time, jazzy stuff. Blues jazz. And it was all right, slide guitar and stuff. It was okay. But we decided we wanted to be a four-piece and we didn't want these other two in the band, so what we had to do was say we were breaking up, then break up, then form again, just the four of us. And then we started rehearsing for gigs, just doing old twelve-bar blues.

"Geezer had never played bass. He was a guitar player before. He didn't even have a bass! So he was playing on this guitar, a Telecaster. And then he borrowed a bass with three strings on it off a friend. Then we had a gig and we borrowed this guy's cabinet. And then we swapped his guitar for a bass, and we went off from there."

Ward recalls this embryonic moment: "I had been playing with Tony since I was 15. We were in local bands, playing pubs, little clubs, maybe, if we got lucky. We were already stepping out to the YMCAs. These were big things at that time. Tony was already experienced, too. He'd been playing in all kinds of bands. So me and him had this kind of getting-together/falling-apart thing, but we always stayed in touch, because that's the way it was at that time. It was almost like it is in Hollywood today, where you kind of get together. It's what I call apprenticeship.

"I remember the first time I met Ozzy. The three of us went over to his house – Tony, myself and Geez – and we knocked on the door and there he was. He had no hair [it was cut short at that time], which kind of turned me off straight away, because I had hair down to my ass. So he said, 'Oh, I'll grow my hair out.'

"Ozzy had put advertisements in the newspaper. He was looking for work. He wanted to be singing in a band. And then I think he called himself Ozzy Zig, for whatever reason. It was a really stupid advertisement. And I can remember, at the time, Tony having some dread when we arrived at the house, because he *had* gone to school with Ozzy. They'd known each other since they were eleven, and Tony went, 'I hope this isn't the Ozzy that I think it is,' and it was. We were going, 'Oh no, we might as well just walk away from this straight away,' because Tony was pretty handy back then. We were very rough around the edges, so I didn't know if a fight was going to break out or not."

The dye cast and the wheels set in motion, they decided to kick it around. They actually played eight or ten gigs as a six-piece, and Bill remembers, with a smile, that these were actually "fun" get-togethers: "It was a real fun band, but I don't think we had a bass player at that time. I think Geezer was playing rhythm, because he had played rhythm in Rare Breed."

If the drummer's first introduction to Osborne was a bit on the skewed side, his initial meeting with his future bass player was little less than *A Clockwork Orange* inspired: "I first met Geezer when he was in Rare Breed. I met him trying to climb up a wall. We used to play the all-nighters back in Birmingham. You could play up to five gigs a day, at least, and this was the all-nighter. I'd been playing that night and I was backstage in this really shitty place, sitting on a couch, and then this crazy person walked in and started to try to climb up the wall. I hadn't seen anybody looking like this bloke. I mean, The Beatles were setting trends – there was attitude and clothing and all that stuff; there was an awful amount of stuff going on – and this person walks in. I was a little laid back, a little loaded, and I remember saying to him, 'What are you doing?' And he said, 'I'm trying to climb up this wall.' And this was my immediate reaction: 'I've got to get to know this fucking person.' So that's how I became attracted to him.

"So, like I said, I believe Geezer was playing rhythm at that time, and I think we did about nine gigs. We did a weekend of different gigs, had good fun up in Carlisle. We went up with six men and we came back with four. That band then became Black Sabbath."

During its short life, this sextet – including Vic Radford on guitar, Michael Pampney on bass, Iommi on main six-string and Ward on drums and vocals – danced beneath the banner of The Polka Tulk Blues Band, thankfully shortened to Polka Tulk. Apparently, the moniker was stolen (borrowed?) from a local Pakistani clothing store, the Polka Tulk Trading Company. Then, in a decision that probably took no thought whatsoever, the band changed its name to Earth. Like their predecessors, Earth were working out on blues numbers such as 'Dust My Blues' and those sorts of I-IV-V songs. Ward described the sound as "earthy, almost jazzy". Even Ozzy had worded his original advert in such a way as to imply that he was seeking a blues-based outfit. English blues during the mid and late '60s was a glorious and golden era, and there was a heaven's worth of material to choose from and be influenced by.

"I think John Mayall was a big influence in England," says Ward. "And, you know, this was where Cream were coming from, The Yardbirds, Jimmy Page way before Zeppelin. So this was, like, offshoot stuff going on in England. It was The Beatles doing their whole thing. Jimi Hendrix had arrived. Johnny Kidd And The Pirates were just about to leave us. But, in the middle of this somewhere, there were these offshoots of blues-orientated bands. And then bands like Jethro Tull, Jon Hiseman's Colosseum, The Keef Hartley Band and others came in. Chicken Shack, with Christine Perfect, who then became Christine McVie [with Fleetwood Mac]. Mick Fleetwood was showing up. So there was this offshoot of music that was going on back then, outside of the pop realm, outside of The Searchers, outside of The Hollies.

"So The Rest were a band that formed when we were at school. And, when we left school, we decided to do gigs. We were doing all Top 40 gigs, trying to make a living. We would sit in solitude, thinking about the music that we really wanted to play. It was just beautiful to play gigs. Shoot, we were kids, just 16 or 17 years old, then."

With enthusiasm in abundance, did the band make any worthwhile compositional statements? "Um, it was okay," concedes Bill. "We were pretty young. We were learning how to play. But we did need a lead-guitar player. Vic Radford was a very good rhythm player, but we felt that we needed a lead guitar player as well. That was the first time I met Tony. I think I was about 15 years old. We found an ad and went over to Tony's house, Vic and myself. He was in Park Lane, Aston, his mother's sweet shop. When we got there, this big guy showed up. He seemed like a nice enough person, and we said, 'Well, can you play Chuck Berry?' He had a white Stratocaster Fender and he had been playing no more 30 seconds and I went, 'Oh, my god!' He was the first real player that I'd ever played with. He could actually play the guitar. And I'm going, 'Oh, my god! Oh, my god!' Tony joined the band and we just got a lot of work straight away 'cause we had the new edition. We had Tony."

For many patrons of the passion of rock, this period – the mid '60s through to the early '70s – was a golden time, an epiphanous moment when the world sought out a new voice, a virgin amalgam of electronics and energy where the monstrous power created by a single guitar as it resonated through a Marshall 4x12 cabinet wedded itself to the primal and poignant pleas of the singer. Like an intoxicant of the worst type, the more you listened, the more you craved. Cream, Led Zeppelin, Traffic, The

Rolling Stones, King Crimson, Yes and 100 other bands were as babies in the cradle seeking their own voices, crying and moaning and screaming and beseeching someone, anyone, to listen.

This is an era now long gone. The motion of our lives was given tempo and rhythm by the records placed on our turntables. Maybe contemporary CD buyers are able to map their own timelines by the plastic they purchase. I hope so. I hope this is true.

"There was a boom going on," describes Ward, an inhabitant of the Camelot that was England during the '60s. "That was created from everything that was coming out of Liverpool. Liverpool had opened up this enormous market, so most of the cities – Birmingham, Newcastle, London, Manchester – all had bumper crops during the '60s. There were a lot of clubs opening up that had never before existed. Everybody was getting involved. There was the general theme of revolution and moving into new directions in a way that had never quite had the strength. I think rock 'n' roll prior to '61 had strength and it had a good thing going on, but I think, when a lot of the earlier rock 'n' roll artists were asked to curtail their actions, it was almost like a Big Brother kind of added cut in what was allowed back in the late '50s/early '60s. I think then, to a certain degree, it split rock 'n' roll somewhat. It was a diminishing of what we knew as rock 'n' roll.

"And so this utterly new phenomenon arrived which was extremely strong. Of course, The Beatles were the forerunners. In Birmingham, literally everybody was in a band. Everybody was doing gigs. Every club was doing five or six gigs a week, so it was very healthy. There was a lot of work and there were lots of opportunities to see musicians and to see what was going on. But there was also a lot of weeding the chaff from the wheat, because a lot of bands were being real safe; they were more or less identifying with what had come out of Liverpool, creating their own version of that and doing that theme, or doing what was current, which was like a peace theme.

"When I was a kid, maybe about 15 or 16, there was lots of stuff to do and take in, because it was starting in America, too. We'd already had a little bit of Frank Zappa And The Mothers Of Invention, and that was something completely new. There were different things happening.

"We were going through the influence stage, but there was something inside that was waiting to come out and it was calling to me. It was Bill, the creative Bill, brand new. I hadn't really been in touch with him that much. That was Bill in the Sabbath days."

Bill's inner voice, the id or the odd or whatever theorists call it, was coming to life. Like a negative in a panful of chemicals, colours were sharpening and ideas were fleshed out. The drummer man was finding his own language, and a large part of that vocabulary had been learned and input somewhere around 1963 or 1964, during a very special evening listening to another quartet of some note.

"Yeah, The Beatles. I saw them when I was very young. I think I was 15. I'd been playing even before I'd heard of The Beatles and before they wrote 'Love Me Do'. I was already tinkering – the school band, theatre, things like that.

"I didn't actually see The Beatles in Liverpool, but I was in Liverpool during my last holiday with my parents. We were in this place called Southport and I could sense there was something going on in town. I didn't know what it was. I could just smell it. There was a tremendous activity in the city. I remember returning from Liverpool as a young teenager, going back to Birmingham and feeling really, really depressed. Birmingham seemed completely dead. It was gloomy. In Aston, we had these little gas lights – we didn't have electric lights or anything like that – so we went back into that dark after the brightness of Liverpool. My brother saw them first and then I saw them, and I flipped out. I was totally entranced by the sound."

3 And On The Seventh Day, God Had A Drink And Created... Black Sabbath

During this period of transition from Polka Tulk to Earth, the band was aided and abetted by a local entrepreneur/musician (jazz trumpeter) named Jim Simpson. Simpson provided guidance, and in fact the band recorded a tribute song to him titled 'Song For Jim', an obscure ditty showcasing Iommi in a rare Wes Montgomery mood. Simpson landed them some gigs at Henry's, a local club, but when they were booked as Earth a rather angry mob voiced its displeasure.

"We got misbooked for them at this venue," cites an amused Iommi. "When we turned up to play, I arrived at the door and we were, like, a little scruffy, fringe things and all that stuff. These guys were there with these bow-ties. They said, 'Oh, you're the band, eh?' And we said, 'Yeah.' Everybody had bow-ties on. And the guys say, 'Oh I like your new single.' Oh great! We hadn't got a single at that time. So I said, 'Oh, thanks. Great.' Of course, it didn't take us long to find out what they were on about. By the time we got inside, we got furious when we realised they booked the wrong band, 'cause we're seeing all these people with bow-ties on and stuff. To keep a long story short, we played and we died a death. They hated us. They were expecting a dance and we were still doing blues stuff. But it was after that that we started writing our own stuff."

Fearing another riot due to name confusion, the band adopted Black Sabbath as their signature. Some members say it was taken from a 1935 Boris Karloff movie of the same name; someone else says it was due in part to Geezer's fascination with author Dennis Wheatley, a spinner of supernatural tales, including his most well known, *The Devil Rides Out*; and still somebody else maintains that it was derived from the song of the same name. (What comes first, the chicken or the road?) In any event, the Astonians rode under a new flag, but money and true recognition were still a genie's wish away. To keep them in guitar strings and tennis shoes, the boys took on day jobs – Bill worked in a rubber factory, Ozzy in a slaughterhouse, Geezer undertook accountant's work (and thus became the band's money man) and Tony futzed around in a number of low-paying and even less gratifying positions.

But a real metamorphosis took place when the group adopted this stygian signature. They had been sharpening their artistic skills at numerous Midlands clubs, in Birmingham and Carlisle, and even venturing across the Channel to perform at the Star-Club in Hamburg, the same site as that at which The Beatles honed their Liverpudlian lances. The band, believe it or not, even broke the Fab Four's attendance records. We can believe in destiny or fate or angel's dust or not believe at all. It really doesn't matter. What does bear discussiong is the almost instantaneous change in the foursome's sound and attitude once they became Sabbath.*

Had the band been waiting for this moment? Was the moment holding its breath, waiting for them to mature and finally hit upon their real potential? Again, does it really matter which came first, the egg or the omelette?

Ozzy tries to sort out the ingredients: "We got sick and tired of all the bullshit – love your brother and flower-power forever, meeting a little chick on the corner and you're hung up on her and all this. We brought things down to reality. Our songs had real things behind them, which I think people wanted at the time. People must have been wanting to hear something real for a change. We don't go out to say that we're the best musical or technical band in the world. We're just ornery backstreet guys who learned to play guitars, drums, sing and things. And we're just making a sound which is free suburban rock, if you like. Slum rock. I don't know what you can call it. There's been so many different bags we've been put into. Perhaps it's the way our environment evolved our minds. It was always a sort of beg-and-borrow trip in life. You always wanted something. Fulfilment. You always really wanted something badly. You were in need of something."

The band had been kicked around, spat on, looked down on and left for dead. And then there was the dream.

★

* In an interview that this writer took part in with Led Zeppelin bassist John Paul Jones back in 1977, the Englishman spoke of the group's first reheasals in awed tones. He knew that they had transcended the mere musical to touch the truly magical. Sabbath members talk about these initial writing/jam sessions with the same reverence.

"A phenomenon happened to all of us, and this is how we came about wearing crosses," describes a clean and sober Bill Ward. The misconception revolving around the wearing of these crosses is herewith cleared up. "In a period of one week, all of us had had the same dream. Neither of us had shared it, because I think we were just embarrassed. Neither of us told each other. I think it was late at night. We were in the van and I think somebody was a bit upset about the dream and they started to talk about it. I just got a jolt down my back because then the dream began to evolve, and I just went, 'Holy fucking shit! The same fucking dream!' Then everybody joined in and everybody admitted it. We had a visitation. And this was kept very private for a long, long time.

"I know Ozzy's father, Jack, reacted to the fact that we were all getting together, that we were working hard, and he recognised that. He recognised that there was something going on here that possibly he couldn't understand, but he knew it was real. He was probably seeing Ozz doing something really real for the first time in his life, and so he made four crosses of aluminium at work and we wore them. Then, suddenly, it was like [snaps fingers] that was it. It was almost like a reaction from Ozz's father to say, 'Hey, you take care of big Ozz,' knowing that there'd been some kind of phenomenon going on here that nobody was quite sure of.

"When people ask me about how it worked, the writing and so on, I haven't told you about the fifth member. The fifth member of Black Sabbath was whatever the phenomenon was, because a lot of times we didn't write the fucking songs at all. We showed up and something else wrote them for us. We were conduits. We didn't even know what the hell we were going to play. We'd sit down and then we'd literally write something. We'd maybe make a couple of changes afterwards. I didn't know that we were going to write what we did and neither did anybody else. We just did it.

"So a lot of the songs on the first, second and third albums were literally songs that were jams. We would put some work into them, but it was almost like that – one, two, three, right there."

Hocus-pocus? Mumbo-jumbo? Speaking in tongues? What's important here is not the answers but the questions. How do you create a sound which might not only make the world revolve in reverse but also take you on an expedition which no drug, drink or dream might even approach? They had been tinkering in a four-track studio off London's Tottenham Court Road, thanks to Simpson's string-pulling. David Platz, another around-town character, fronted the band £400 to make an album. Simpson was shuttled aside to make room for producer Rodger Bain while he scooted about the city in an attempt to drum up interest. They woodshedded at Hamburg's Star-Club.

Simpson, an avid jazzologist, played 78s by such artists as The Count Basie Orchestra, and drummer Ward admits to the influence: "Yeah, I was brought up on that, 'Philly' Joe Jones and Louie Bellson and Gene Krupa. If you listen to the structure of Sabbath music, you'll hear Gene Krupa. He's in there. On 'Wheels Of Confusion', I go on bass drums and toms. It's the natural place to go. So I'm driving the toms and bass drums. You've got to know where to reinforce it, where to feel it. The first song on the *Black*

Sabbath album, 'Black Sabbath', that's a typical song where most of my work is done on toms. I swing a lot. On 'War Pigs', I'm swinging at the beginning, playing in swing time. Actually, on 'Black Sabbath' I'm playing in swing time, too. And I used to use real big cymbals, about the biggest you could get."

What made Sabbath such an intriguing group of players was the manner in which they didn't play. They had neither the sheer musical excellence of their Birmingham neighbours Led Zeppelin nor the face-punching bombast of The Who. They made up for this lack of instrumental mastery with the simple application of orchestration and ensemblification.

Bill, turning a fern-like shade of green upon hearing his close friend John Bonham's trap precision on Led Zeppelin, relied on jazz chops to make the rhythm section sound fuller: "Geezer plays orchestrationally, and so do I. I don't play drums. Not one of these songs do I play drums on. In the late '70s, there was precision rock. They were playing drums, and I classify those people as drummers, but I don't classify myself as a drummer. To this day, I still don't classify Geez as a bass player. I think he's a bloody poet. That's in my world. I've always thought the only musician in Black Sabbath was Tony Iommi. That's nothing judgmental about Geezer's playing or anything – he's a fabulous player, the best player I've ever played with – but to me, he's a poet. And he's an Irish poet at that, even though he was born in England. He's from Irish descent.

"Our music was orchestrated. When I play with Tony, I don't think it in drum time. When Tony would play a lead, I would react – angrily, emotionally. So he plays something to me and I'm not even thinking about that lick. What I'm doing is painting a picture that will work behind it. Where's the right place to drum? He can play whatever he's going to play, and it's like I immediately react."

Like a chain reaction, the music being churned out was having a profound effect on audiences. In the same way that Ward sensed this fifth presence while composing early Sabbath pieces, crowds were being wound up, adrenalised and exploding in a myriad of emotional and physical manifestations.

Ward, sensing a revolution when first scoping The Beatles, was equally moved by Sabbath's early performances: "I saw everything changing in front of me, in terms of crowd reaction. In blues situations in England, everybody would sit down and just kind of nod. Now they weren't. At concerts, kids screamed. Now something new was happening for the first time. People were showing up with chains and leather, holes in the ass of their pants. I saw it change right in front of me. It was a new thing that was happening here. It was small at first – tricklings, small followings. Then it dawned on me that a whole new generation of attitude, art, design, texture and clothes, a whole new thing was fucking emerging here. And it was plugged right into our music. Because I wasn't aware of anything else at that time, any other band at that time, I knew what was going on in music at that time, and I saw it growing. I saw it happening right in front of me. There were people just the same as us showing up with standard shoes, sneakers, jeans, leather jackets, T-shirts, and all these people were... They call them headbangers now, but that was the beginning of headbanging. Headbanging started in the clubs, through Ozzy. We were rocking out and we wouldn't let anybody sit down. That was a no-no. Suddenly, everybody was up in the clubs and we were rocking. I'd never seen anything like that before in my life."

4 Sing A Sab Song

Besides the brain-smashing now taking place at virtually every regional Sabbath gig, the band were slowly making themselves known outside the Birmingham area. Slowly, ever so slowly, they made their way southward to the big time of London. Their appearance still intimidated a lot of people, because by this time most other bands had cleaned up, cut their hair and donned suits. "We looked like we'd just arrived from Seattle," jokes Ward. Add to this spectre a band that played at above tolerable decibel levels and you get some idea why they had such a difficult time in landing a record deal.

"We were very, very loud," says the drummer. "And also, nobody knew what was going to happen. We didn't know what was going to happen from one beat to the next, because we were so spontaneous. So, if we didn't like something, we would stop. Ozzy would yell and scream. Sometimes, I'd just walk off, throw my fucking sticks down. It wasn't unusual to throw drums at the audience or jump down into the audience and get involved in some fights. But this was 1969. We would stop playing if somebody was getting hurt in the audience and get it sorted out. That's where headbanging began.

I saw the leather genre begin there, because we used to have leather jackets, kind of like those early Beatles photographs, back in 1961 or 1962. We were a very undisciplined band. I never knew what was going to happen on any given night."

On one evening, when the band were supporting Jethro Tull, guitarist Tony Iommi was approached by mentor/leader Ian Anderson. Mick Abrahams had just left the band and the flautist was in need of a new member. Tony left Sabbath to join Tull and even appeared in The Rolling Stones' *Rock 'n' Roll Circus* film, but ultimately he paid heed to his original calling and came back to Sabbath. "It just wasn't right, so I left. At first, I thought [Jethro Tull] were great, but I didn't much go for having a leader in the band, which was Ian Anderson's way. When I came back from Tull, I came back with a new attitude altogether. They taught me that, to get on, you've got to work for it and get up and rehearse. Somebody's got to be a leader of sorts; you can't just get everybody to go, 'Well, we'll make it at some point and rehearse.' You have to have somebody go, 'You've got to be here at ten in the morning and get cracking.' I was put in the spot of leader, really. They looked to me for that guidance, and I got the band work. It was because of Bill Ward and myself, basically. When we first started this line-up, we worked up north, because nowhere else would have us."

Bill Ward, too, has that evening fixed in mind. On that particular night, a conversation took place. "Ian saw Tony playing and approached him about that. Everybody interacted back then. The houses where we were playing, these large public pubs, had facilities for about 500, 600 or 700 people. Everybody was there drinking and there was that kind of atmosphere. This was about 1968 or 1969, some of these shows, and we still didn't have much of an audience then, but little by little we started to have our own following. We were supporting a lot of acts back then like Tull and Keef Hartley, and even Ten Years After."

Alvin Lee, an early and staunch supporter of the band, was instrumental in helping them find gigs and even assisted them. "He took an interest in the band," says Bill. "Back then, he was enormous in what you'd call the underground circuit. Ten Years After were a very popular band. He hadn't done Woodstock then, but when Woodstock happened, he really became 'it'. He was very popular on the London scene and we visited him at his house and even wrote little press clippings in the paper. We got Alvin's seal of approval.

"Ian Anderson said the same things. We first met Tull in Birmingham, and they were late for a gig, so we'd been playing and warming up for a while. Ian and Mick Abrahams came in, and when they got on stage they said, 'It seems like the band you were listening to right now seems to be doing a much better job than we could have done, anyway.'"

This new work ethic, combined with the band's more intensive dedication in developing original material, finally paid dividends. Upon Tony's return to the fold and the almost simultaneous name change from Earth to Black Sabbath, they secured a record deal with Vertigo in 1970, after more than a dozen rejections. The label, an offshoot of Phonogram, also signed Juicy Lucy and Manfred Mann's Chapter Three. During the final weeks of December 1969, the group was working in Germany and Zurich, and even with a major signing the money they were earning was still laughable, some sets garnering a mere £25.

They returned to the four-track facility on Tottenham Court Road, and among the first songs they wrote under the new deal were 'Wicked World' and 'Black Sabbath'. The band's namesake song, that three-note gem that became a must-learn lick for every burgeoning electric guitarist, took form instantly. The fifth member, maybe, wanted his cut of publishing.

"It's funny," says Tony. "That song just sort of came. It's really strange. I never sat down and worked it out or anything. It was just one of those. I'd get into rehearsal and they'd look at me to come up with something. That was always the way it had been. They'd sit there and go, 'What are you gonna come up with?' I just turned it up and played and turned down. I started playing with it and it sounded good. They liked it. We just built it up from there, worked on it. We needed an end, and it just sort of happened. It just fell into place. I didn't work it out before; it just happened there. As a matter of fact, a lot of stuff happened just like that, on the spot.

"And they'd go, 'Oh, what about this?' I wouldn't know what I was going to come up with and I'd go, 'Oh, what about this?' Because that way you're going to come up with something. It makes you think more. I'd just come up with these riffs as though I knew what I was talking about. Most definitely not! I didn't know what it was going to be."

"'Black Sabbath' was a bass lick," adds Geezer. "I didn't want to win medals for how fast I could play, how many notes I could play in one millisecond or anything; I just wanted to play riffs on the bass and not stray off the main thing."

And Bill, ever the philosopher, glues these observations together with a splash of Elmer's insight: "Back then, we all left each other alone. Tony would do whatever he wanted to do because, if he was happy, then he was happy. No one got in on each other's stuff. We just used to say, 'Well, that sounds really fucking good.' We complimented each other whenever we were happy with each other. I'd get a 'Well done, Bill' if I was trying to grab something, some weird timing or whatever. We just had our songs. We went into the studio and played them. It was exciting, being in the studio. It was, like, our first time. It was a big thing."

With the band working with a budget somewhere between £400 and £600, *Black Sabbath* was completed – astonishing as it may seem – in two days. In the main, these tracks were sliced, diced and spliced in such a rapid fashion because the recording was essentially live – that is, guitar, bass and drums were exhaling sounds simultaneously, and then the recording was played back to check if any fix-it work was required. All of those seminal albums released during this frame of time – the late '60s/early '70s – were executed in similar fashion. Zeppelin, Hendrix, Cream and Jeff Beck were all captured on tape with only a modicum of overdubs.

It's for this reason that these records, to this day, stand

as champions among the tons of garbage subsequently released. Knob-diddlers and monkey-see/monkey-do record producers sacrificed the heat and the drama created when three or four musicians, burning it down together, captured that invisible, intangible "thing" and transferred it to tape. The later philosophy tended towards overkill, doubling and tripling and greasing down guitar and vocal parts to the point at which character was eliminated and the use of ever-more-complex recording consoles became *de rigueur*. This first Sabbath album was completed on an eight-track machine. Eight tracks! But, as is human nature, an attempt was made to improve on the original, and, like the tail chasing the dog, all that came from the "glorious" advent of technology was more tracks, less artistic identity and a general clogging of the aural arteries.

"We try and create the same kinds of things live as on the album," reveals Iommi, breaking it down to the basics. "We don't like to go in the studio and be strict. We just go in and play like we do on stage. There's no strict routine. It's always been in that sort of flowing thing. I mean, the first album was done in a couple of days. We just went in and played.

"We knew at the time that it was something different, but we didn't know if people would accept it. We didn't know what people would think, but at that time we were satisfied. We were pleased with it because it's how we felt when we made that first album. And it was so close to us that we just hoped people would like it. It was a bit of a step, something different, thinking about supernatural things."

Ozzy, too, sensed that there was a newness about the album, a sound and sentiment never before explored. But it was precisely this wild and untamed frontier for which they were heading that made the record such a heart-pounding and brain-expanding work: "For its time, we didn't realise the stuff we were writing. We just thought, 'Well, let's try it this way' It was purely four guys from the back streets of Birmingham saying, 'Let's have a go. Let's do something really heavy and rough.' There was no smoothness. There was all the rough edges, just banging it out and seeing what happened. And that's what people out there wanted. I mean, if you're a Pink Floyd fanatic, don't come and see Black Sabbath. If you're an Ozzy Osbourne fan, don't go to see Pink Floyd. It's just a different variety. Honestly, I think that record took twelve hours to record. We just went in and played it and then put it out."

There was actually a single released about one month prior to the February 1970 sale of the album. The seven-inch 45 contained 'Evil Woman (Don't Play Your Games With Me)' (actually a cover of a song by a band called Crow) backed with 'Wicked World'. The single stirred up just a minimum of curiosity in the band, although the album *Black Sabbath* would eventually rise to Number Eight in the British charts and Number 23 in America (on the Warner Bros label).

Not enough may be said about this debut, although Tony makes an attempt at summing it up: "We thought, 'We've got two days to do it, and one of the days is for the mixing,' and we thought that was a long time, so we played live. Ozzy was singing at the same time on some of the rhythm tracks. We just put him in a separate booth and off we went. We never even had a second run of most of the stuff, 'cause they said, 'That's it. That'll do. Next song.' We never thought any different. We'd go, 'All right. Okay.' I'll never forget when we come to do 'Warning'. It's a long song and I did that guitar solo in it and we thought we were going to have to redo it. And I said, 'Well, I didn't like what I played. Any chance of doing it again?' And they said, 'Well, you know, okay, we'll try it again. One more go. If you don't get it this time, we'll have to use that one.' And that's how it worked. It wasn't like we could drop in stuff here and there. It was live.

"I think that was really part of the magic. You had to do it *then*. That was it, you know? If you made a mistake, well… And, of course, 'Warning' was quite long, and they couldn't fix something that was wrong. I still felt I could do better, but they said, 'No, that's it.' But we didn't know any better. And sometimes, when you're trying to recapture something, it doesn't always happen."

At this time, another Birmingham band were conjuring their own source of blues wizardry and, about a year prior to Sabbath's record, had given birth to their first child. *Led Zeppelin* was a blueprint, a road map, the secret passage to Valhalla for an entire generation of Les Paul-wielding guitarists and Alps-yodelling vocalists to follow. Although their music bore little if any resemblance to Sabbath (beyond the obvious physical format of instrumental trio fronted by singer), many people felt that it was Jimmy Page, Robert Plant, John Bonham and John Paul Jones who deserved the title of original head-smashing architects. But Bill Ward, a very close friend of Bromwich-born Bonham, denies this. He is not reluctant, however, to make known his feelings about his drummer buddy's first album.* It should also be touched upon here, before we hear from Bill, that the two were also frequent drinking companions, and the death of Bonzo on 25 September 1980 weighed upon Ward like a large – and sometimes visible – blue elephant.

"I grew up with John, and me and him had traded licks and played together since we were 15. When he was doing the country gigs, sometimes I'd end up supporting him. [Zeppelin and Sabbath never performed on the same show.] Sometimes he'd support what band I was in. We were always crossing paths in those days.

"Zeppelin were a blues-rock band. They were a whole different ball game. They had acoustic things going on. Robert was singing about being in love. We were talking about Vietnam, war pigs and everything else, and we were talking about, what is this that stands before me? There was rage in our music and there was never any, as far as I'm concerned, of this fucking myth shit that we seemed to get blasted with, all that demonic crap.

"But I remember, in the middle of a lot of Sabbath gigs, it was very busy. We were heading up to Carlisle, and one night somebody put on this album, *Led Zeppelin*. And we listened to it, because we knew John Bonham and we knew Robert Plant, so it was, like, 'What are they up to these days?' It was Zeppelin's first album, and

---

* In fact, it's also worth noting that Zeppelin, like Sabbath, were absolutely trashed by the press. The media also insisted on defining Page and company as "heavy metal". Toss out this term in front of Jimmy in describing his music and you'll be lucky if all he does is turn you into a toad.

I put it on and we went, 'Holy shit. Oh, my God!' There was some envy there – they had an album out and our album wasn't out until some months after theirs.

"So Zeppelin went in on the ground floor, and my biggest fear was – and it was a selfish fear – that, at that time, we were going to come out and the press were going to have a field day, because Zeppelin were going to clone us. John Bonham and I played really aggressively and really loud, but we'd been doing that for a long time, so at first I felt a little bit like, 'Fucking shit.' In any event, it worked out that we were both in completely different places, anyway, so it didn't make any difference. And I can hear Robert Plant saying, 'What competition? There ain't no competition when it comes to us,' you know, 'cause Robert might say something like that, God bless his little heart.

"Shit, I can remember me and Johnny drinking together, fucking chugging Johnny Walker. We've had people come up and say, 'You two fuckers are gonna be dead in fucking five years if you don't cut it down.' Fuck. We had people telling us that all our lives.

"I knew John had the capacity of a horse to drink. I know that he drowned on his own vomit – at least, that's what I was told. I was in bed when I got the news. I was loaded. I hadn't seen the daytime for maybe a week or two. I think I got told the story by the dealer, who was actually one of my dealers, a big fan of Zeppelin's. He came over and says, 'Bonham's dead.' And my first reaction: 'Yeah, and I'll be next.' The very first thing that came out of my head. 'Yeah, and I'll be trailing right behind you, John.' But Bonham's death also made a significant change in me, because it put the fear of God in me. When John died, I just went, 'Holy shit! We can die.' It jolted me, in the sense of saying, 'I'm going to be next.' But I was saying to myself, in another sense, 'I don't want to be the next.' So I was very, very sad. And I will always speak highly of John Bonham for the rest of my life."

Things were changing. Reality was setting in, and England – much in the same way that America had been rebelling and revolting against the norms and accepted ideals during the '60s – was now about to stand before this same precipice. The Beatles had opened the doors, but any throughway was meant to go in as well as come out. Zeppelin were scrambling their own sounds, shuffling through Page-arranged blues and bluesing their way through updated shuffles; Jimi Hendrix made everyone take notice; and when Black Sabbath turned it up another notch, the teen kingdom was ready and waiting for a new English family to lead it through the rubble into its own sort of wasted-land.

"It was just that time, I guess," speculates the drummer. "It was time to have a Black Sabbath. I think God wanted a Black Sabbath. It was okay to have another family offshoot, because there was a big musical tree going on, and so it was time to have another part, another branch, a very strong branch, which is still, to this day, going on. Twenty-six years of this branch growing. I think it helped when Keith Moon kicked his drums over, and I think it helped when Cream performed. All of that was very important. When Jimi Hendrix sang 'Hey Joe' and when Dave Davies played out of that amp that gave him 'You Really Got Me', all these things were permissible. When The Beatles did *Sergeant Pepper*, it was all becoming allowable.

"And what came from that was a grungy little band. In England, grungy means dirty, a dirty band. What came out of all of this was this grungy little band from Birmingham that was influenced by all that stuff. And all we did was simply turn up. We had the cumulative anger on stage. It was unbelievable. All the anger came out of us. We were really aggressive. That's what was being performed: the anger.

"I think there have been some very creative hard rock bands over the last 26 years who have all formed their branches, too. We just happened to be the first band that did that. I think we made it possible. I'd like to think that sometimes my drumming was so simple that it made it possible for the kid on the street to say, 'You know what? I can do what Wardy's doing then. He's only doing this, for God's sake.' I tend to think my drumming was reachable by the common man, because my drumming is very, very simple. I'm notoriously out of time. I'm not ashamed of that at all. I'm a notoriously bad timekeeper, which is not very good when you're a drummer. You see, the more I let myself know that, the better timekeeper I became. I can talk the truth about myself, so I'm not going to hide in some flim-flam, wishy-washy bullshit thing. I know that my timekeeping sucks, so when I allow myself to say that, it gives me room to grow from that point. But you've got to admit it first."

5 In The Black

With the release of the band's first album, money was a little more readily available. Not much more, but at least there was payment for food and the odd new garments of clothes. All four members had lived a life if not necessarily at poverty level then certainly one without many embroideries.

In fact, even after their debut release, Ward's parents still refused to believe in what he had created. His mother, if the truth is told, was a supporter of her son's desires, but Mr Ward the elder would never truly embrace Bill's art. This may explain why, later, the drummer attempted to numb – indeed, destroy – himself in a toxic tornado. "My father would not accept the reality of what I did until I visited him in hospital with the album *Black Sabbath*. He was very ill at the time, and that's when he let go. He couldn't stand to see my work. He cried. His words were, 'You're ripping yourself to pieces.' He couldn't stand it. He was never able to. He only came to one show, at Birmingham Town Hall. There's a picture on the inside of *Volume 4* where I think all my hair is sprayed, and there's a picture of us on stage somewhere and Geezer's got that silly checked coat on. We played

Birmingham Town Hall on several occasions, and my dad came to one of my gigs there, but he never came to another gig ever again. He couldn't stand to see me pulling myself to pieces. What I mean by that is that I put so much aggression and so much energy and force into my drums. He couldn't believe that I did that every night.

"He knew that I loved music, but he could not face watching me do that. It was uncomfortable for him, whereas my mother loved it. My mum came to a lot of the gigs in England. She was there on stage. Oh, God, yeah, the mums would come to the gigs."

Ozzy Osbourne's upbringing also played a large part in the person he would later become. He indeed worked in a slaughterhouse, as did Bill Ward's brother, and was already taking drugs such as speed at an early age to make the conditions at least bearable. He also did time as a plumber's apprentice and worked on an assembly line testing car horns at the Lucas factory.

He saw no real opportunities there and took to a life of crime, breaking and entering and committing various other misdemeanours and felonies. He should have remained in the slaughterhouse. He was caught and spent three months in prison, where he gave himself his first tattoo, a needle-and-graphite operation. On his release, knowing that he couldn't go back to a factory job, he put up the famous "singer looking for gig" sign. From that point, Ozzy began playing with Geezer and then, eventually, Tony and Bill.

"We used to jam together and play a few gigs together and we wrote original music, and it worked," theorises

Osbourne. "I had gone to school with Tony and I was working in a semi-professional group with Geezer [Rare Breed]. Then we all formed and met, and we chose Black Sabbath as a name. I mean, we didn't plan it and expect it to make such a profit as it did. It's just one of those great things in life. We tried to put music over in a different angle. It had an evil sound, a heavy doom sound. And then there were all these fucking witches and freaks phoning us, wanting us to play at black masses and all this crap."

Iommi continues the story: "As soon as the album started selling, we started making money We were always doing another album, doing live dates. We weren't thinking about, 'Oh, how much money did we get?' The money just came in and we didn't even see it. It went into the company and that was it. We didn't really think about it. I think the first album was in the charts in America for two years, in the Top 100, which was surprising to us, because we never knew how it was going to go."

During this period, the band were beginning to involve themselves more heavily in drugs and alcohol. Everybody in the band was drinking and taking various forms of Quaaludes and then potent variations of hash, but these recreational devices never seemed to get in the way of the music. Tony admits that the band members were great friends during the making of these early albums: "Things were fine. Once we got past the small things, the band together was fine. I think Ozzy was always a little bit worried, but it was good for him, because it gave him a bit more, you know? I'd always go, 'Come on and get it going, Ozzy. It's time to go on. Tell a joke or something.'

He would go on stage and he didn't know what to do or what to say. I wouldn't know what to say, either. Organise a raffle or something. That was our objective: we'd organise a raffle."

Ozzy did come up with the Richard Nixon arms-raised-in-victory peace salute. Osbourne did handle his stage antics. In the year of the first album's release, the group graduated from club dates to outdoor and festival shows, including two festivals at Plumpton with King Crimson, Julie Driscoll, Roy Harper and Ginger Baker's Airforce; the Hollywood Music Festival, including Family, Ginger Baker (once again), The Grateful Dead, Mungo Jerry and Colosseum; and, in Munich, the Euro-Pop Festival, appearing alongside Free, Rory Gallagher (a close friend of the band), Atomic Rooster, Status Quo, Deep Purple, The Edgar Broughton Band and Black Widow (another band emerging at the same time as Sabbath and using the realms of darkness as their main musical themes).

When Bill Ward is questioned about this period of big outdoor shows, his memory is less than excellent. His drinking had escalated tremendously by then and accounts for these absences: "I don't remember much of any of these shows. I do remember a place called the Plaza Hansworth, where we played with Pink Floyd – that was owned by somebody called Ma Regan, as in Mother Regan, but we called her Ma Regan. She had four ballrooms. Floyd were playing and they had two Transit vans and we were supporting them. I think we were the first band, then there was another band and then it was Pink Floyd. It was trippy, you know, 'cause they used this scaffolding even then, these fill lights and their little stage show. And then you said there were festivals in Plumptown and Munich and the Hollywood Music Festival? God, I don't remember any of them. I do remember we played with Rory [Gallagher] a few times. I do remember playing the Royal Albert Hall, later. I knew it was a classy joint. We got banned from there, and then they let us come back. Then we got banned again."

The first album was selling well, bigger venues were being offered and the time seemed right to start work on a second record. The band were feeling a sense of power, as if they'd been touched by something other-natural, not necessarily something evil, but that fifth member was present. *Paranoid* was recorded on a 24-track desk, and by this time the band had much more room for experimentation and exploration. But there were repercussions still resounding from the first album and these darkened themes. Iommi elucidates: "I think from day one, when the album was done, particularly in England, the inverted cross on the outer sleeve and the front-cover pictures with a woman there were obviously to go with the name of the band. It brought all other things with it as well. And people were thinking, 'It's all Satanic,' which was understandable. I mean, that was the image that was presented. As far as the record company was concerned, they didn't really know us, and when this album cover was designed, that's the way it was done and we liked it. And, of course, we didn't see the inverted crosses until a later date."

And what would the band have done had they seen the reversed crosses?

"Well, we didn't have a lot of say in it, at that point. They were the marketing people. But that's what started the image of the band. And with the songs, I suppose, they were our darker side. But some of it was the dangers of the darker side. I think that, when the first album came out, people were very frightened of us. A lot of people wouldn't even talk to us, because they really were fearful of us. I didn't know this for a long time. We found this out later. Some people would say, 'God, we were really frightened to meet you, and we're quite surprised, now we've met you. It's not like the way we thought.' I think Ozzy felt the same way about it. I mean, yes, we liked the idea of what's beyond, but as an interest. Certainly in no way as the practice of such. And that's as far as it went, really."

Following the birth of Black Sabbath, the band abandoned the management leadership of Jim Simpson and went with Patrick Meehan and Wilf Pine, a pair of make-it-happen music figures who had previously worked for Don Arden (another figure to cross the band's path at a later date) and left that nest to work with the band.

Just to re-cover our tracks briefly, in December 1969 the band signed to Philips Records subsidiary Fontana and, in the following month, put out the debut single 'Evil Woman (Don't Play Your Games With Me)'. It did not chart. In April 1970, the song was reissued on Philips' new "progressive" arm, Vertigo, but still failed to make any dent whatsoever.

Then *Black Sabbath* hit the stores, after being recorded in just two days, under the production ears of Rodger Bain. It ultimately made its way to Number

Eight in the British charts and remained in the listings for five months.

The band then began working on a second album, *Paranoid*, which would eventually be released in January 1971. The title track and 'Iron Man' are probably the two songs that best represent the band: full of monolithic guitar licks, lyrical venom and that unique scream/moan unique to Ozzy – not really a musical motif in any sense of the word but dripping like an overripe plum with attitude and angst. 'Iron Man' was the band's only song ever to enter the US charts. The album was king of the hill in England and made it to the lofty position of Number One. Like the first album, this one was despised by critics. It made no difference. Sabbath were becoming established as a group, breathing the same elitist air as Zeppelin and Purple.

"I think we started to get a little bit of a different sound," Ward announces of *Paranoid*. They now had 24 tracks on their desk to noodle with and more than two days in which to fill them. "We were getting better all the time. And that first album was selling, too. We had just enough people in England buying it to put it in the charts."

But every up had its down. Ward continues, "I think there was a sense of power when we started to get Number Ones. But then we started getting banned from places. There were riots. We went through Sabbathmania – police escorts, the whole thing. When that happened, I felt a very dangerous sensation. It's very dangerous because it's an illusion but it exists at the same time. And I also felt a sense of safety, a sense of okayness and a sense of power, although that's a dangerous place to be for too long. And I think I naturally passed through it. We all naturally passed through it and settled down. I've seen many bands go through that when they're breaking. There's a lot of adulation."

Again, all of these prizes – the adulation, the power, the money – had a price, and many of Sabbath's contemporaries – John Bonham, Keith Moon and others – never made it to the other side. "In recovering from rock 'n' roll, there are several things that have to be done," says Bill, as close to a casualty as anyone could become. "One of them is to recover from yourself and realise that you are not there any more. People like to stay there because they feel safe there. It's very difficult to let go of that and be vulnerable and let yourself be here and now, take risks and do all kinds of weird things. Passing through that can be painful. Some of my friends are much older now but they are back there. They have not let go. It's very sad."

Much has been said about the relationship of drugs/alcohol and rock 'n' roll. The names of those who have succumbed are on all of our lips, but what makes Black Sabbath such an intriguing study is that all of them are still with us, breathing bodies and thinking minds.

Writing began for *Paranoid* and, in Ward's words, "We were being closely watched." The group wrote while on the road but, as with their debut album, the compositions came pretty quickly. When Bill is questioned about his main memories of those writing sessions, his answer is a one-word response: "Drugs." Hashish was now the mind-number of choice. Many of the songs were written in the Aston Community Centre, a small recreation/ rehearsal facility the group rented out for about "a pound a session".

The group was also well aware of the turmoil happening in America – the Vietnam War, the individual versus the industrial complex – and they addressed this situation on the track 'War Pigs'. A song like 'Hand Of Doom', meanwhile, was completely out of character for the group, since it addressed – intimately – their use of drugs. Music journalists despised the record, but what really touched Bill was the way in which Tony Iommi was treated as a non-player. "What hurt me most about that critique was the fact that Tony was such a damned good player and still is such a damned good player. It's like, God, okay, slag the band if you have to but give this guy some credit here, you know? And Ozzy worked his ass off every night. So did I. So did Geezer. We worked really, really hard. We didn't fuck around with this thing. We were a hard-working band. And at least credit that, even if you don't like the music. The music was very misinterpreted in the early years."

Although Ward was a staunch supporter of the band's music, as they all were during these salad days, Ozzy was not bent so much in defending the band against criticism. Granted, he bit the heads off various types of fowl and pissed – excuse me, urinated – on the Alamo for reasons only he might know, but these statements came after he left the band. Please do not misinterpret these statements – Ozzy Osbourne lived, breathed and came close to dying because of his love for the band; but, as in any group of people, cliques spring up. People find more comfort in the company of certain individuals than others, and a slight shifting of power is continuous. Late in 1995, Ozzy, about to begin another solo tour with Joe Holmes in the guitarist's seat, spoke a little about these early feelings: "To be perfectly honest with you, Tony Iommi and I never really were very close. I went to school with Tony and I was in a band with Tony, but we never really socialised too often. I mean, Geezer is with this new band I have now, and it's great to have him. I've always been in a band with Geezer, even before I was with Tony and Bill. [Tony] always had a barrier around him. I never, ever really knew him.

"After the No More Tears tour, we started to go chasing around the Sabbath reunion idea." (More on this in later chapters.) "I had doubts about it, but I thought, 'Well, we don't have to rehearse much, just go in and brush up the songs and then do the shows.' But, as the negotiations went further and got deeper and deeper, I suddenly realised that you can't rekindle that. Everybody had a manager and everybody's manager was doing their best – and so they should – but it brought up the old saying, 'Too many chiefs and not enough Indians.' It's just like a relationship – as you go on through your life, you always remember the fun parts, the good parts, and then you condense that down. Say you have a relationship for a year, and in that time the real good, fun parts can be narrowed down altogether to one month. Forget the eleven months of fucking misery. I would think, 'Oh, yeah, that was so much fun when we did that.' You forget the two weeks in between on the tour bus when we were travelling and fucking feeling miserable, homesick, full of the flu or fucking fed up with singing 'Paranoid', fed up with doing drugs and waking up with a fucking hangover."

What about the money involved in a reunion tour of the original Sabbath people?

"Well, I was personally offered a fucking small fortune. I mean, I'm financially okay, but I don't turn down money if it's there. But in my heart, it wasn't right. For the first time in my life, I was actually having long conversations with Tony Iommi. We talked and thought maybe something good would come out of it, but in the back of my mind I just felt something terribly wrong. I didn't feel terribly happy. I suppose that the situation as it was when we were together – having a rapport with Tony and living the way we did – maybe that was the reason why Sabbath worked in the period of time that I was with them.

"Don't forget, it wasn't only for the years that I was with them that they were successful. The *Heaven And Hell* and *Mob Rules* albums were pretty successful. I never listened to anything [Sabbath recorded] after I quit. When I first left the band, it was kind of me versus them, but as the years have gone by, I'm older and a lot wiser now. If they're making the next fucking *Thriller* album, good luck to them."

Geezer, too, knew that it was no bed of roses dealing with the band during the making of this second and subsequent albums. He swore, on more than one occasion, that he would never play with Ozzy again. And yet here he is in Osbourne's new band. How does he explain this?

"It's fun," Butler admits. "I mean, you go on and have fun every night. The songs are classics in their own right. [Several Sabbath hymns are included in the set.] With Ozzy, it's off and on between me and him. We've had nasty fights and haven't spoken to each other for two years, and I've probably said at least three times, 'I'll never play with Ozzy again in my life.' And then, you know, time goes by and we start talking again and get together. It's just one of those sorts of relationships.

"I have a song on my album [Butler's solo record titled *Plastic Planet*, released in 1995] called 'Giving Up The Ghost' about giving up that whole thing. Originally, the album was going to be called *Giving Up The Ghost* and the whole band were going to be called Giving Up The Ghost, too. [They're now called g//z/r.] I was sober, and that's how I felt about the whole thing, at the time. It was just the disappointment and the frustration and the fact that Sabbath now had absolutely nothing to do with the old Black Sabbath, apart from one member. [Tony Iommi.] And when I did the last Black Sabbath tour, I was embarrassed that the band was called Black Sabbath. Especially now that the band have got this legendary status. It's impossible to live up to that. You talk to the kids and other musicians and they just don't have any respect for people going around calling themselves Black Sabbath. People were saying that to me when I was in the band: 'Why the hell do you keep going on as Black Sabbath? You're not Black Sabbath.' And I realised that it wasn't – it isn't – Black Sabbath. It was just going down and down and down, and I wanted to get out of it before the name was totally destroyed. Now I'm trying to give up the ghost. That's where the song came from."

Here is the lyric: "You bastardised my intellect, castrated our conviction. You are desperately seeking Satan, now that you've burned your bridges down. You plagiarised and parodied the magic of our meaning. You can't admit that you're wrong. The spirit is dead and gone. You don't bother me. You are history, a legend in your own mind. Left all your friends behind. No one seems to care and Satan is not there. There's nothing left to boast – time to give up the ghost. You are desperately seeking Satan. Black magic has turned to dust. It's time to put the thing to rest. You can't admit that you're wrong. The spirit is dead and gone."

In relating to the time-frame revolving around *Paranoid*, Iommi recalls quite clearly what the writing sessions had devolved into: everyone else popping down to the local pub while he floundered and twisted under the extreme pressure of preparing material for the all-important sophomore album. While Ozzy and Geezer may be harbouring ill feelings about Tony's continued usage of the name Black Sabbath, perhaps it is the guitarist as much as anyone in the band who deserves to keep that banner waving. The left-hander's memories leave little doubt as to the original source of the material which would become this second album: "In those days, I shared songwriting and publishing with everybody, but until I'd come up with anything, nobody would do anything. They'd got to a stage where sometimes, later on, right before we were doing the *Never Say Die* album, they'd all walk down to the pub and leave me in the rehearsal room trying to come up with a riff! Then they'd come back two hours later and say, 'Got anything?' What the hell? They thought of me as a machine: 'Did you come up with anything?' I'd say, 'Oh, yeah, I've got this idea. What about this?' And they'd say, 'Oh, right, okay. Well, we're going to bed now. We'll try it tomorrow.' They were too drunk, man.

"There was a lot of drinking, around that time. Later on, when we started touring, we were trying acid. We weren't really into it. I think Geezer has done it, but we weren't too much into it, just uppers and downers and Quaaludes, whatever you like. And then it got to the stage where I was coming up with ideas and forgetting them because I was just so out of it. You know, what was that idea I had just done? I forgot it."

With the advent of 24-track recording, Iommi was thrilled with the new sounds that he was developing. Years earlier, he had snipped the ends off two fingertips while running an electric welding machine. He was certain that his career was over, but in fact this digit diminishment provided a major part of the style that he would go on to create. "You see, I can't use right-handed instruments now," he points out in his October 1974 *Guitar Player* interview (the only feature ever written about him in *Guitar Player* and conducted by this author), "because I snipped the ends of my fingers off and on [a guitar like] a Les Paul you've got to get right up to the end of the guitar, on a reversed right-handed instrument, to hit the strings. Not many people know about the accident. It happened years ago, when I was doing electric welding. One day, I had to cut this sheet metal before I welded.

Somebody else used to do it, but I had to do it this day because he didn't come into work. There was a faulty switch or something. *Thhhhht!* I pulled it out and it just gripped the ends [of my fingers] and pulled them off."

As fate would have it, on that very day, he was due to leave for Germany to work with a rock outfit. Feeling completely lost, he decided to give up the guitar, until a friend bought him a record by Django Reinhardt. After hearing what the master gypsy guitarist did with just two fingers, Tony again took up the instrument and slowly activated the two clipped fingers, along with the two healthy ones. "I had to start all over again, which was kind of a drag. I have to wear things now because the ends are so tender. It's helped me a little, because now I use my little finger a lot." These prosthetic devices are essentially small plastic thimbles that fit snugly over the ends of the guillotined phalanges. They allow the finger a normal length. Although he has gone through a series of other devices, nothing has provided him with the dexterity and natural feeling of an intact finger, but he has turned this tragedy into a sound and style completely Iommi-esque. Still, there have been bouts with severe frustration, resulting in poor performances and even violent episodes: "I'd get annoyed and pick the guitar up and smash it."

Fingers shortened and tempers heightened, Iommi managed a tone no one else could create. Opening up his true feelings, he's certain that no one knew just how difficult it was to cope with this shortcoming: "At first, I don't think people realised how hard it was to learn to play like that. It involved a lot of determination and a lot of hard work and practice. [The accident] happened around 1966, way before Sabbath or Tull, and when I joined Jethro, they even said, 'What are those things on your fingers?' When I told them, they were quite surprised to find I could play guitar. I've had to adopt a totally different way of playing because of these fingers. I mean, it's much easier when the flesh is there, as it should be. Now, instead of, say, pulling a note, I have to sort of push it up to get the vibrato. These tips are a bit clumsy, and they slow me down and get in the way. I even have to wear leather on them to grip the strings. But it's something I just had to try and overcome.

"That changed my whole life. I mean, I thought I was finished. I really thought it was the end. I had to come up with something to make me play again. It was a very difficult time to relearn everything and try to play again. You know, you're used to playing chords quite ordinary, but everything was different. But when you do something like that, you think, 'Oh, I can't play that chord now. [My fingers are] going to split up and bleed.' So I had to make the thimbles. I had to come up with a surface that would slide and just slip off and rip the string at the same time. I had to make them myself, because nobody was around there to do it. And then I had to work on a whole new technique. I changed to light strings. I couldn't use heavy strings, 'cause you have to bend them, and that hurts. Then I got into the whole guitar thing [of] digging the frets down and polyurethane on the necks – 24 frets and on you go."

Regardless of his hand-y-caps, Tony was stretching the band. Subtle though it may have been, he was pushing the quartet into more orchestrated music, exploring dynamics and taking his influences – people such as Jimmy Page and Dave Davies – to create a new texture. Black Sabbath's Midlands mates – players like Bonham and Plant – were true supporters of the band, and on more than one occasion some wonderful moments transpired. Bonham, as we've already established, was a serious drinking partner of Ward, and this led to some memorable times. It's important to cite these brief passings of time, since John is no longer here and his interaction with Sabbath sheds a different light on the character he was.

"Like I said, I've known John since I was 16," enthuses an exuberant Ward. "He was in The Carlton King Snakes. We were both in bands doing our own loading out at night and it was always, like, 'How you doing, Wardy?' And I'd say, 'Doing all right. How are you?' We traded licks. He had a killer bass-drum sound when he was about 16 years old. His bass drum was unbelievable.

"He'd got thrown out of this club. It was only me and him in the club – we played the same night. His band were on first and we were on last. John set up his traps and… [laughter] He was doing these soundchecks with the bass drum and bouncers came up and said, 'You can't play like that in here,' so they threw him out. The rest of the band hadn't even shown up, which gives you an example of how loud it was, that bass-drum sound.

"But we weren't particularly good to each other when we were drinking. John liked to drink and I liked to drink and we were rude to each other, but we still remained friends. We stuck to each other, you know? He'd put his arm around me and I'd put my arm around him, and he was probably thinking, 'Yeah, fuck you,' and I was probably thinking the same thing when we were drinking. But, when we weren't drinking, I thought we were very respectful, very professional, congenial friends. It was nice. We had mutual respect for each other.

"John was a big fan of Black Sabbath. His favourite song was 'Supernaut' [*Volume 4*]. He loved it. Robert [Plant] and John would come into the studio and play the song. John loved to play double bass drums, but to my understanding Robert and Jim didn't want him playing double bass drums. If you listen to John, he could do it on one bass, anyway. So that was my understanding, or at least that's what John shared with me. In his words, it was something like, 'Them bastards won't let me use two bass drums.' That's the real stuff, right there, referring to Mr Plant and Mr Page. But he loved it. And he openly envied me, 'cause he would get really pissed off that I was using two bass drums. He would call me an asshole: 'You've got two bass drums and I haven't.' So, when he came in, whenever we were around or whenever it was possible, he would play on my kit and it would sing. He would make the kit sing.

"And he loved to do 'Cornucopia' [again from *Volume 4* and a track that almost resulted in Ward's dismissal from the band – more on that in a later chapter]. He'd play that song with Tony and Geezer. He liked to play 'War Pigs', too. He liked what I did with the hi-hat. But he was always jiving me about how I had too many drums and said, 'These bastards won't let me have any drums.' There was a lot of rivalry, but it was a good friendship rivalry. So that's Mr Bonham. I miss him dearly, to tell you the truth."

Obviously, Bonham and Ward had little in common as players: the former kept time like a Swiss clock while the latter, by his own admission, couldn't keep time if a metronome had been hotwired to his aorta. But it was this rivalry/friendship that made these years during the early and mid '70s so critical to the music that followed. Styles were being forged and, in his own way, Ward developed a sort of sloppy coolness that has gone on to touch trappists in many of today's contemporary combos.

Bill, however, did see the other side of Bonham:* "I have to respect John Paul [Jones] and Robert and Jim, but I know that John could be very rude. I had a drumming relationship with John, the same way Geezer had a relationship with Robert Plant, with Bob. But there are some things which I feel need to be kept private. It belongs to them. It's their stuff."

In the meantime, *Paranoid* was taking shape. Like other bands of the time – Zeppelin, Pink Floyd, The Who – alcohol and drugs did play a part in the development of this second record, but in Ward's words, "We didn't sit down and go, 'Well, let's get really loaded tonight and then we'll come up with something really good.'" The substances were available, and a by-product of the ingestion and upending of bottles was the creation of

* In 1977, this writer went on the road with Led Zeppelin for nearly two weeks, and when Bonham was drinking – which was most of the day and night – he could be profoundly mean and rude and not someone you would want to deal with on any level. This addendum is only inserted to provide a fuller character study of someone who was arguably one of the most ground-breaking drummers ever to have played. Drinking or not, his performance night after night was an unforgettable experience.

these sounds. Sometimes the band was chemically altered, other times not. In other words, they were not consciously aware of making supposedly "drug-orientated" music.

Originally, *Paranoid* was to be titled *War Pigs*. The band, as has been alluded to, was aware of the turmoil taking place in America and felt the title fitting. In the end, however, *Paranoid* won. Although some people may think that it was Ozzy who contributed the bulk of the lyrics, in truth it was Butler who acted as the central source for words and phrases. The band were a democratic unit then, and all decisions were presented for vote. Ward's take on Geezer's verbal dioramas seems worth noting: "Geezer would write [lyrics] and Ozzy would write them and we'd sit down, would listen and go, 'Yeah, that's cool. That's okay.' Ozzy is an interpreter. He breathes in the music and spits it out, and I think that's his greatest gift. He's just so incredible like that. A lot of the time, you would look at the lyric and go, 'What the fuck is this about? What the fuck are you writing here?' And that's the truth of it. If you listen to a Sabbath song – 'Supernaut', for instance – the first impression is, 'What the hell is he singing there?' But Ozzy would digest it. He'd have to digest it. Sometimes he would be laughing his balls off. I don't know how sensitive Geezer was, but to spend so much time on a lyric and then to have it kind of laughed at, it's something to think about. I really wouldn't like to be in a position of writing up a bunch of lyrics, taking it to somebody and them going, 'Hah hah hah. What the fuck?'."

The title track was a true team effort, realising a final shape and arrangement in 20 minutes. All of it was written in the studio. This was the miracle, the phenomenon of Ward's fifth member, that basic idea of the whole being stronger than its parts. "That was the fifth member, yeah," remembers Bill. "It already had the songs written. We were just the conduits. I mean, we literally came into the studio and Tony was just being Tony, and he just started to play. Luckily, somebody had the tape on. We just sat down and were just looking at each other, kind of going, 'Well, what the blazes do we do now?' We didn't have enough songs for the album, and Tony just went [sings 'Paranoid' guitar lick] and that was it. We'd been playing so long, too, that we could play off each other. It took 20, 25 minutes from top to bottom."

Whatever amount of time it took to write the songs, the band found themselves with a Number One record in the UK, while the title track leapfrogged to Number Four. Released in December 1970, the album would perch itself in the British playlists, and in March 1971 it would reach Number Twelve on its release in America and remain in the charts for 65 weeks. This carved out a strong US niche for them and prompted an almost mandatory tour.

Their remembrances of this time are vivid. What confronted them were new horizons – vast, untapped and, until the band arrived, unspoiled. Like their Birmingham mates before them, Led Zeppelin breathed deeply of the (back in the late '60s) relatively clean air, the pure and seemingly endless supplies of nose sprays, pills, gel-tabs, mind-alterers and enhancers. Sabbath were no different. They had a killer album in the charts and the country, like a ripe fruit, awaited their tasting, sucking and digesting. Their maiden tour in autumn of 1973 presented them with a palace of sin, a skeleton key for every door and the abracadabra with which to unlock any chastity belt.

A large part of their success in America rested with the journalists. Although American writers, like their English counterparts, seemed to delight in denigrating and downsizing Sabbath's creative drive, they were nonetheless enamoured with this uniquely British approach to rock. For every negative review, promising sentiments were rising from typewriters across the country.

Sabbath was not instantly digestible. Like Zeppelin, they required years of understanding from the press, although record purchasers knew instantly that the music was something remarkable. Years later, they were finally honored with the *Nativity In Black* tribute album, and magazines that had initially snubbed them gave them premier coverage.

In the June 1991 issue of *Guitar World*, the magazine placed *Paranoid* in the Number 16 slot of the "25 Greatest Rock Guitar Records" article. Even then, the editors had a difficult time in giving with one hand without taking away with the other. The editorial in its entirety reads, "Even those who find the distinction a dubious one must acknowledge that Black Sabbath are the founders of heavy metal. The band's dark and weighty influences transcended many musical boundaries – as well as any semblance of good taste.

"*Paranoid* is quintessential Sabbath. Tony Iommi's riffs – big, sludgy and dipped in demonic swill – helped fashion 'War Pigs' (the greatest HM song ever) and other timeless classics, such as 'Iron Man' (featuring opening riffs to make your molars abscess) and the colourful 'Rat Salade'."

This is a positive review, mind you. Here is a portion of a swipe originally appearing in *Rolling Stone* and poison-penned by Nick Tosches on 15 April 1971. This is the day by which tax returns must be submitted in the States. Maybe he owed money to the Feds. He couldn't exactly aim his wrath at the IRS, so he took a vituperative shot at Sabbath: "They shoot 'M' and they engage in group sex. No act is too depraved, no thought too bizarre, as they plunge deeper and deeper in the realm of perversion, into the ultimate 'trip' of their own self-fashioned Hell. Orgies, incest, drugs, homosexuality, necrophilia, public nose-picking, Satanism, even living sacrifice."

It's difficult to believe this paraphrasing of a review which reduces these four to less than murdering, Nazi-crazed Limeys drinking blood instead of four o'clock Earl Grey. And it's not true. No one has ever seen any of them pick a nostril in live performance.

Again, with the benefit of hindsight, the group's music is still appreciated. In a 1992 issue of *Guitar World*, in another "Top 50 Heavy Metal Albums" piece, the group's music is cited: "*Paranoid* sneers at everyone else from its Number One position. This time, there is no give/take – it's all give.

"[This is] the album that defined metal, musically, sonically and thematically. Hate-mongers ('War Pigs'), lunatic robots ('Iron Man') and schizos ('Paranoid') dance a jig while Sabbath's four horsemen of the Apocalypse play instruments of mass destruction. The star of the show is Tony Iommi's detuned SG, which pukes the largest, loudest guitar sound known to man. Add Geezer Butler's sci-fi lyrics and Ozzy's prophet-in-the-wilderness vocals and you have the rock equivalent to the book of Revelations [*sic*]."

They also nailed position Number 16 with *Black Sabbath* and Number 44 with *Heaven And Hell*, so if the Yanks weren't ready for Sabbath, the Blacks were primed and cocked for America. "We came over and did our first dates at the Fillmore," Iommi draws from a long-past memory. "I don't think we were headlining; I think we came over mainly doing shows with Mountain. Leslie West. It was really great. We did some gigs on our own and some with Mountain, and then we came back a second time and headlined. Then things really started going for us. We played the Fillmore East and it was the first time we'd ever used a good sound system. That first tour, we did bring all of our own sound system, which was absolute rubbish, compared to the things you get over there. We used Laney columns, speakers and amplifiers at that time. It was great to be able to play with monitors and use mics. We'd never used mics before! We never had anything. It worked really well and we loved it. Then we did the Fillmore East with Rod Stewart, and that's when we realised we were getting quite popular, because they were booing Rod Stewart, and we thought, 'This is happening for us.'"

This brought the group to a higher level – for the first time, they had the luxury of utilising monitors. One of the first dates was a two-night set at a small club in New York, when all the equipment blew up because the mains supplied the wrong voltage. Tony thought, "Oh God, is this what it's going to be like? A six-week tour of *this*?" But they then played the Fillmore and the electric gremlin was greased. By their second tour, they were headlining.

6 Once, Twice, Three Times A Crazy

The band returned to England and started kicking around ideas for their next album. With crowds screaming nightly for the anthemic 'Iron Man' and 'Paranoid', the group knew that they couldn't stray far from these primal and instantly gratifying gut-wrenchers. They recorded in England and shifted studios several times in order to find the essential location. One reason for the change in sites was Ward's inability to lock into a particular track. (Iommi seems to recall 'Lord Of This World' as the culprit.) After a time, though, they ended up at Olympic Studios. But in those days, studios were seen merely as buildings housing recording gear and they really gave little thought to how important a multitrack establishment might be in actually improving the sounds of their records.

"I think it was just really very basic," an honest Iommi relates. "You just went in and used nothing where, later, if you went into a better studio, you'd think you'd have a better studio and better facilities [so the sound would be better]. But it doesn't always work like that. We started doing that, and the more we started using better studios, the more we'd get involved in messing with things and it would take longer, because somebody would want to use this new gadget in there and it would take us longer to do it. We got more into the technology side of it and we started spending more and more time in the studio. So that album, *Master Of Reality*, we did all in London."

This album attained Top Ten positions in both UK and US charts, climbing to Number Five in the former and Number Eight in the latter. The music was Sabbath unbridled, rotund riffs supplying background to Ozzy's monotonish mumblings. 'Solitude', the ballad of the lot, was somewhat reminiscent of the low-key pieces appearing on the albums by American West Coast troupes *à la* Quicksilver Messenger Service and Jefferson Airplane, and one wonders if the group's sojourns to the US left any residual effects. Drummer Ward shoots down the theory: "Actually, I was very out of touch with those two bands. I was pretty much caught up in Black Sabbath, by that time, and I wasn't really hearing much of anybody else that I'm aware of now. We just went in and played around with these things."

And what about the hacking sounds at the intro of 'Sweet Leaf'?

"That was very necessary to do at the time. Letting people know about marijuana – that's what it's about. As a matter of fact, that cough on the front is Tony coughing. He'd just had a blast on the pipe before we started. We recorded it, man, and we just rolled."

'Children Of The Grave'?

"I liked that song very much," continues Ward. "I used a timbale thing. I did the movement with my left hand and played the drums with my right hand. That was one of the first major overdubs of the day, 'cause we didn't overdub on *Black Sabbath* or *Paranoid*."

This was a relatively major step forward for the band, but they would make even larger strides on *Volume 4* and, particularly, on *Sabbath Bloody Sabbath* (1974) and *Sabotage* (1975).

"I don't recall me doing one single drum overdub," Ward said of those first two records while involved in one of his own projects, *When The Bough Breaks*. "Maybe a tambourine would have been about it. So coming to *Master Of Reality* was like, 'Whoa! I'm going to do a drum overdub? Wow!'"

Because *Paranoid* produced such an enormously profitable egg, there was a significantly bigger budget to deal with for succeeding albums. There was therefore more experimentation in the studios, and the natural end result was more overdubs and aural tinkering. Looking back, Bill realises, "Studios were changing and we were getting into nicer studios. We had a bit of a following now, for sure, and we'd had a Number One hit ['Paranoid'] and all that." But the budget was not funnelled entirely into the physical creation of the music; drugs, which had been present even before the band began to record together as this entity known as Black Sabbath, were becoming even more prevalent, and now there was a briefcase full of cash with which to purchase these pheromone developers.

Bill, long since sober, confesses, "Yeah, we were getting into coke big time, and we were going into real professional big studios, so it was like putting kids in a candy store. It was like, 'Oh, my God.' So we started to learn, 'Oh, you can overdub. You can double-track that. You can drop in that. You can pull out that.' And compared with today's studios, it was quite archaic stuff, but it was still more advanced than what a lot of the bands had the benefit of doing already. There were a lot of bands that were recording in these incredible studios at the time, and now we were getting inside that, too, so I could do a drum overdub."

But the band still felt itself lying on a bed of nails. Critics found little to their liking on this third album and, combined with the group's increasing dependence on cocaine and hashish and that ever-underlying feeling that they'd better find something brilliant after coming off the supernatural qualities of a Number One record, the lads were beginning to feel the strain. They began to feel the type of pressure most people never succumb to – that hand-around-the-heart sensation making every breath a concerted effort, when those creative angels disappear, when ideas slip down some black hole as vast as the universe and you know that you will never retrieve them.

When we see the aftermath of the horrors visited upon those persons whom we always assumed invincible, some small part of us is vaporised as well and we're separated by a gulf, a stygian gap sucking in thoughts like a crack-crazed addict. We only know these people by the records, seeing them on television, in concert, and there's a certainty within us that they'll live forever. But the originating and procreating and conceiving of sounds and notions and words virginal and unheard and unseen is a process so debilitating and consuming that there is a need – or, perhaps, there becomes the need – to feed ourselves with the chemical, the smoke, the powder, the prayer that we hope will bring these muses fluttering once again to land upon our shoulders and speak to us in that language so very few are able to understand. Running a corporation? Performing brain surgery? Running a country? These are all profound endeavours, but there are trails through these jungles – books, experiences, other people. The answers are there.

For Black Sabbath, for Led Zeppelin, for The Beatles, these substances are conduits to souls and forms of expression lying so deep within the ephemeral that no book, word or sphere in this world holds the answers. So the deaths of Jimi Hendrix and Keith Moon and John Bonham and Janis Joplin and Elvis Presley and that personal list we all carry within us is a result of the bird which no longer visits. It is the guitar left unstrummed, the sheet of music paper untouched, the melody remaining unsung. And when that tiny (for some obscure reason they seem atom-sized) gnome finally reappears and tells us what to sing and which words to write, he/she exacts a toll. Depression. Drug abuse. Suicide. Death from the unknown stranger who will never know true creation and hence feels the right and, in some truly twisted situations, the obligation to snuff someone else's candle.

So *Master Of Reality* was a beginning and an ending. Money, tours, unadulterated adulation and unqualified success had come their way, but this bird does bite and, although it has been mentioned once and will be touched upon again, it is a marvel that Black Sabbath did survive, albeit somewhat the worse for wear. This particular go-round, those names were not on this list. Ward, who has held hands with the Reaper, tries to put this section of time in some perspective: "I almost want to say that it was a resolved thing, or the ending of something. In *Master Of Reality* – at least, in my opinion – the band started to feel very fatigued, very tired. We'd been on the road non-stop for year in and year out. We were constantly touring and recording. I can even remember a conversation that we were having when I think we were heading down towards Heathrow Airport to go back out on the road one more time, when we all just admitted that we were plain exhausted. We were just gone. So I think that was the end of an era, the first three albums, and somewhere along the line I think we decided to take our time with the next album, which was to become *Volume 4*. Originally, I believe it was to be called *Snowblind*, but that was unacceptable for the record company, so it got changed to *Volume 4*. There was no *Volume 1, 2* or *3*, come to think of it, so it's a pretty stupid title, really.

"But I think, at that point, we had decided to ease off a little bit. We decided to give ourselves a little bit of splendour. We got nice places in Beverly Hills and we recorded the album at the Record Plant, although I think we did take some of it back to England."

Ozzy, too, was not oblivious to the strains and pulls exerted upon them following the chart-shattering results of *Paranoid*. As if echoing Bill's impressions of that era, his thoughts are terminally barbed with drugs and double-tracking: "*Master Of Reality* was the turning point. That was the last real Sabbath album, as far as I'm concerned."

If fact, Osbourne had grown so unhealthily consumed by the lifestyle that he even invoked the idea of quitting the business entirely. Years later, when his own solo career was well established, each tour was definitely, and without question, his last. His most recent outing he dubs "the Retirement Sucks tour", a nod to the inhuman wounds inflicted upon the artist by the music and its machinations. "And then we started to progress into *Sabbath Bloody Sabbath*, where we started to get mechanical in the studio, using synthesisers and then overtracking and double-tracking and triple-tracking and backward cymbals and standing in the bathroom with a bag of coal in your mouth. I call it the investigation period. It's like the guy who invented the fucking thing that couldn't stop growing." That bird of insight which lights upon your forearm, whispers the next lyric into your ear and then leaves behind a bite mark like that of a rabid fruitbat. "For instance, the first albums were the quickest albums and they were the biggest-selling albums of Sabbath. The later albums took forever to record and they didn't sell really anywhere near that. There's something in that, you know? If you've got a tune and it's lively, if you work on it, it's like you have a record player and you hear the same song every minute of the day for three months. You'll fucking hate it. You'll think, 'Jesus Christ!' At one time, every song on the radio sounded like The Eagles, and it's at a turning point where I think everybody just sort of got Eagleitis. It's overkill.

"That was the last album we used Rodger Bain for.

Then we used Patrick Meehan on *Volume 4*. But we really didn't have much to do with the production of those records, anyway. All we did was put these cute little effects on. You pushed the buttons and we played the music. The production is one side of it, but if the music is strong enough on its own, if it's got the vibe, it'll go anyway. All you've got to do is get an equal balance."

Any Sabbath/Ozzy fan has his or her own identification card filled in with the statistics that they truly believe make up this undeniably unique singer. One of the reasons why the band were able to continue for so many years with the original line-up was because they had achieved a balance, a sharing of power and powders and passions. Some may think that Ozzy stuck up a 2x4 index card on the local Aston bulletin board and landed a gig. We've spoken about his work with other bands, and if you look honestly at the world of music as it revolves today, there are few artists continuing to sledge out essentially head-thrumming music and making a living. Ozzy Osbourne had and has a unique vision of what he wanted, and Black Sabbath was his birth passage into the rock world, and he's not one to forget it, although he does toss insults and garbage at it: "Professional? No way. Forget it. [That was] the first fucking lunacy that I was ever involved in. It did have its great moments, but Sabbath became like a dinosaur – it got too big to fucking survive, 'cause we wouldn't come down to the terms. We thought we were too good to do anything – like Zeppelin, like Pink Floyd had reached that niche where they could record and not go out on the road, because they were like the invisible band, but when they came out, it was like, 'Phew!' Like God had arrived. And Sabbath were blinded by the fact that they thought they should have been there, but we never quite got there, because we weren't prepared to put the hours in that the other people did. Zeppelin went on the road for fucking three years before they could even bother to do that or even afford to do that, where Sabbath went on the road for a six-week tour on, then three weeks off. We'd stop here or there, take a break. We were the biggest hypochondriacs you'd ever met in your life. We must have spent most of our earnings on doctors' fees. It was like, 'I've got a pain.' 'Go to bed for three days.' It's just fucking indigestion from eating too much Chinese food from the night before. Or, 'I've got cancer.' 'Sure you have.' We always said, 'If I die, bury me in England.'

"Bill Ward used to have a bag so full [of treatments]. I mean, it got to the point that we went on the road one time and he even had a snake-bite kit. I said, 'Where the fuck in hell are you ever going to see a snake? Where on this Earth are you ever going to see one? Or are you going to fucking drive to a zoo or something?' He says, 'You never know. Some of these snakes run pretty fast when you're driving across the desert.' [Osbourne breaks into laughter.] On a fucking 650 motorbike, in the fucking Colorado Desert. I mean, if the snake ever bit him, the snake doesn't have a fucking chance.

"We used to call him Dr Bill and Valiums Forever. If you had anything wrong with you, you'd just go and see Bill. He was fucking full of them. He had things for everything. I mean, when he came up with that snake-bite kit, it was like the ultimate. I'd never seen one of those things. He had a big old razor like your dad might have, and I said, 'What if it bites you up the ass, Bill?' He said, 'Somebody's going to have to suck the poison out.' [More laughter.] I said, 'Don't come to me, man. Find a new friend to help you.'"

Ozzy does have fond memories of his first trip to America, and he sees it as one of the "great moments": "I suppose, when we first got to play the big arenas, it was like we went from one tour, played two nights at the Whisky,* and then from the Whisky we went to the Forum,** but I hated playing the Forum. We hated it. It's a weird sound when you're playing on stage there.

"But we used to do a lot of gigs at the Whisky. This is early '70, '71. Mario [Maglieri, the establishment's owner and a key figure in the development of all of the bands listed in *] was there then. The first time I saw Mario, he comes out and says, 'Here's a bottle of booze for you.' And he didn't have to do that. He's really good, one of the genuine blokes in this business. He's always been a nice one. Even when I had a bad period, he'd go to me, 'Have a drink. How are you doing? Sit down.' I mean, he's not one of those guys who says, 'Fuck you,' when you're down. He's done a lot for rock 'n' roll."

What Mario sensed, perhaps, in the quartet was its twisted take on the roots of music. They've all admitted to a fixation with the blues, but it was their distorted view

---

* The Whisky A Go Go, on Sunset Boulevard, in the heart of the Sunset Strip, was a seminal club for British bands coming over in the late '60s and early '70s and was also the launching pad for West Coast bands The Doors, The Byrds, Buffalo Springfield, Love and many more.

** A major arena in Los Angeles, housing around 17,000 people.

of this musical panorama that caught the Whisky owner's ear, as well as the hearing knobs protruding from an ever-increasing horde of young heads seeking that sound, that perverted pitch which ideally would send them reeling. Sabbath were to the blues as Picasso was to pictures – yes, there were brushes and paints and figures spread across a canvas, but Pablo's survey of the landscape was more Venusian than it was Earthbound. His glasses (if he wore them) were not rose-tinted; they were rainbow-flecked and reflected the world as he viewed it. No one else saw those images. But history has him as a genius, a giant among paint-splatterers, precisely because he eyeballed people and places and things around him in a manner no one else ever did. Genius, like God, is in the details, and although his work appears to be technically simplistic, the care with which he developed visages with misaligned eyeballs was the task of a man who saw ever so clearly a world living in the trifles.

For similar reasons, Black Sabbath found a following. 'Iron Man' and 'Sweet Leaf' and 'Snowblind' and 'Cornucopia' were harmonically and melodically mangled pieces which no one had ever heard assembled in that fashion. 'Iron Man' and 'Black Sabbath', though, are guitar chants that we're certain we've heard before, dirges lying within the recesses of our craniums which, when first heard, trigger the response, "Yeah, I've hear those songs before." After all, 'Black Sabbath' was a three-note riff lying around for centuries and during the days of crucifixion and men fighting with swords was dubbed the *diabolus in musica*. The Church would not allow this interval – the flattened fifth, or tritone – to be played within its hallowed walls.

Nothing was taboo by the time of *Master Of Reality* and *Volume 4*, however. The process of choosing and recording material was a democratic one but not one without its share of power plays. If the truth lying in details is one unwritten commandment for the success of a band, dictum number two must be balance. One person laying down all laws is a philosophy doomed to failure. (It's senseless to even name names here, because everyone already knows the list.) Part of Sabbath's survival lay in the band's ability to toss out the oysters and hang onto the pearls. This isn't to say that they weren't blinded by the plastic – hell, everybody backs a loser – but, while recording these groundbreaking albums, and up until members came in and out like a hooker's bedroom, their sense of song predilection was superb. There was give and take.

"By the time of the third and fourth albums," weeds out a discerning Ward, "everybody was working on the music and being an individual. I had noticed it, anyway. Everybody had their own individuality. I thought it had been like that right from the very beginning. So it wasn't a situation of, 'No, I don't think Ozzy loved everything that Tony did.' Ozzy had ideas. There were things which not all of us liked what we had. There were ideas that I might have had, and I can remember many times not having the ideas accepted, which was okay. It was, like, 'Okay, well, I love the guys enough to have that kind of refusal.' And even Ozzy's ideas weren't necessarily accepted all the time. I didn't sense any kind of power play. I know there's always been a leaning towards Tony being the possible candidate as a power player, but I really think that, when we agreed upon something – and I like to believe this as the truth – we were all agreeing upon it because we all liked it, and not because it was something that Tony or Geezer or Bill or Ozz necessarily had to have that way. It was mutually agreed.

"Basically, we were all into the blues – John Mayall, Cream, The Yardbirds, Jimmy Page playing way before Led Zeppelin. I guess a big part of this is the fact that Tony and I spent most of our teenage years together, from age 15 on. We spent a lot of time working together. There were times when he would not be working and I wasn't working, but it was just a convenience thing, finding work with other people. But I knew I was going to be in a band with this guitar player for the rest of my life. I love playing with Tony. We always came back to that. When I played with him, I was spoiled. I had to work, with him, because he was a very good player. He didn't ask me to work harder, but if you were going to play with him, you just did.

"I've always felt him to be a better guitar player than I have been a drummer, period. But one of the things that I can do, being the drummer that I am, is listen to Tony. And this is no offence to my drumming friends, 'cause I know Vinnie [Appice] and I know Cozy [Powell] and I know most of the guys that have worked with him. None of them listen to him in the same way that I do. I know that because of the way they play, the way that they're accompanying him. I accompany him completely different, and he knows that. We've been together for years and years and years, and he knows that I have no time. I freely admit that! I have no concept of time or measurement or anything else,*

* Watch The Black Sabbath Story: Volume 1 (1970-78) and Volume 2 (1978-92), both released by Warner Reprise Video, and this becomes terribly self-evident.

and I'm not ashamed of it at all. It's just a fact. It's just real. So, as he began to venture out into new ideas, I had to work, too. I got tight and I got to be a very, very good drummer – in my opinion – relatively quickly. I worked my ass off. By the time I was 20, 21 years old, I'd reached that place where I could hold my own and it didn't matter who the fuck I was playing with. By the very nature of the person, being around Tony, I wanted to be able to support him well, and that meant me doing my homework.

"I play orchestrationally and I paint pictures. I don't play notes. And I listen to him all the time. Some of his best licks have been when he's not been listening to licks. So I'll just listen, if I'm hanging around, and I'll hear him play something, maybe three notes, and I'll just rush in and go, 'Can you play those three notes again?' And he's, like, 'Oh?' You know, little things like that. Of course, it's coming out of him all the time. It's just listening. But I want to really be careful. I'm really not saying anything bad against these [other] drummers. They're my friends.

"So, growing up with Tony in our teenage years, we grew up fast. We both worked very hard. I need to emphasise that. We weren't sitting on our asses. I knew that, if I had to play with a guitar player, it was Tony that I wanted to play with, because he was the best. He had already got a reputation in Birmingham. When he was about 18, 19 years old, he was leaving most players way, way back. He would accelerate with his playing, and there were some very hot players around back then. One that stands out immediately to mind was Rory Gallagher, a beautiful guitar player. Rory was just a beautiful man, and man! Could he play the blues. But I saw the way Rory did it, with Taste, and I saw the way Tony did it."

Tony did have a profound effect on the band and on Bill, who suggested bringing in a string quartet as a backdrop for 'Snowblind', a track from the *Volume 4* album. Ward even tried conducting this auxiliary quartet. Frustration is the only memory he still carries regarding that adventure.

Influenced as he was by Iommi, Ward changed to a double kick drum set-up for this album. The band flew to Los Angeles to record (the first time they'd make such a migration), and for the first time they weren't guillotined by the critics. Although the band were monstrously successful by this time (the first four records all broke into the Top Ten, reaching Numbers Eight, One, Five and Eight, respectively), the count had started. The rock 'n' ref had begun his tally. The City of Angels soon became the City of Dangers. Temptation was everywhere, and for four young men rising from the working-class environs of a small English town tossed into the centre of the Devil's own den, "No" was a response difficult to utter. Maybe it was the new location, maybe the pharmaceuticals, but here in paradise, *circa* September 1972, history almost unravelled and handed Bill Ward his walking papers.

"We were burnt out," emotes the drummer. "We were wiped out. We had what I like to call '*Beatles For Sale* eyes'. Look at their eyes on that album cover. They're gone. Those guys are toast. They're fucking history. And that was about their third or fourth album. And that's simply because of the fatigue. We were burned out. I mean, that's like a professional boxer boxing every night. Unbelievable.

"So we booked the Record Plant, and it was a progression for us. I'm real critical of that, but I guess it was coming along. Most of the work was done. We'd already got it in place. We kind of knew where we were going. We had tightened up a little bit in the studio, and there was a phenomenon that was going on, something new that had happened in my life at this time: cocaine. 'Snowblind' came from that. Like we said before, the album was going to be called *Snowblind*, but Warner Bros refused. They didn't want that.

"So by now I'd been using cocaine for a while, and it's a 24-hour drug. I was loaded all the time. I mean, hash was always there for me, but I moved into hard narcotics at a relatively early age, and I remained addicted. I mean, I'm a narcotics addict to this day.* At that time, I was abusing that stuff. There was lots of money and nothing to worry about. There were lots of women, by this time, but we all had our wives and had all settled down. I was already on my second marriage. I was 24 and already on my second marriage.

"But something happened there, on this album, which was a little bit rough. We decided to go back to England and finish up some of the work. There's a track on there called 'Cornucopia', and I had a really tough time with that track. It's still a nightmare to me. And sometimes Tony would start playing it, when we got together, to remind me of the nightmare. He knows it was a thorn in my side. I just could not get along with that song. And it got pretty bad. I was nearly kicked out of the band because I was having a tough time trying to play that

* Ward has been entirely sober for many years.

song. We ended up in London, and they were still trying to track it.

"I *hated* the song. I just wanted to play some blues. I just wanted to do some jamming. I felt like we were writing to make the next album or something, you know? Because you can get caught up in that. It's a dangerous trend, riding the gravy train. It's a bad thing. So I was just getting pretty miserable in the studio, and then Alvin Lee showed up. In them days, we knew Alvin pretty good, so I said to him, 'Let's just do some jamming or something.' Me and Alvin were sitting down in the middle of the room, doing some [drugs], and I got some pretty nasty looks from the guys in the studio. We weren't actually jamming; we were doing something else in the studio. I won't share it specifically, because I have to respect Alvin's personal issues. But at this time, it was time to work. It was time to be creative.

"I just had this terrible resentment about 'Cornucopia'. There were some patterns that were just… Uggggh! It was horrible. I mean, I nailed it in the end, but there was just a hang-up about it. The reaction that I got, the cold shoulder from everybody, it was real bad. I went, 'Uh-oh. Am I too far gone? Have I gone too far?' And I was asked to leave, basically. It was like, 'Well, just go home. You're not being of any use right now.' I was getting that message. I looked to Ozz, 'cause usually Ozz would say stuff like, 'Go sit down.' Me and him, we were just like real buddies. But he didn't say anything.

"At the time, I didn't have a place to live in England. I didn't have a house, because we were on the road all the time, so the hotels were where I lived. And that night,

I didn't know what to do. My wife and I were pretty zonked, so we slept on Geezer's back lawn, and I didn't know what to do. I thought I was getting kicked out of the band. I felt really scared at that point. That was the very first indication that there was a change, because that had never happened before. It had all been fine. Suddenly, here in *Volume 4*, there was a change, a definite change. It really scared me. And it was the first time that any band member had ever been rebuked. It hurt. I mean, they didn't want me in the studio. Sometimes we'd have cross words, but that was the first time I actually felt like I'd blown it, like I was about to get fired. That's how I felt. The only person I knew to go to was Geezer. He wasn't too happy when I showed up. In the morning, we were sleeping on his back lawn, with coats over us. In those years, my second wife and I, we led a kind of a *Sid And Nancy** life."

---

* A movie by Alex Cox about Sex Pistol Sid Vicious and his girlfriend Nancy Spungen.

7 The More Things Change,
The More They Stay Deranged

Despite Bill Ward's ordeal with the *Volume 4* track 'Cornucopia', Black Sabbath had the cake, were eating it and even owned the bakery. Once again, they changed management, this time signing with Patrick Meehan. They had Los Angeles in their blood, money was rolling in like the sweet waves of the Pacific Ocean and the world was theirs for the plucking. They had actually committed themselves to Meehan and partner Wilf Pine some months earlier, and this new consulting team had landed them a spot on *Top Of The Pops* alongside Engelbert Humperdinck, Diana Ross and Cliff Richard.

Earned money was being spent. Tony, ever a car fanatic, was filling his garages with Ferraris, Lamborghinis and Rolls-Royces. (They each bought a Rolls – sort of a boys' club thing.) Houses were being purchased and music gear upgraded. Again, though, he who giveth taketh away. As Tony expressed it, "What it came down to was that we could buy whatever we needed. And, because you could do that, we lost a little of our incentive. Nothing seemed to mean anything any more, 'cause we could get it so easy. The challenge had gone out of it."

Complacency poisoned the music that they were beginning to assemble. Perhaps looking for an easy way out, Sabbath returned to America in an attempt to recreate the magic of *Volume 4*. Prior to compiling material for the record which would become *Sabbath Bloody Sabbath*, they released 'Tomorrow's Dream', a cut from the previous LP and their first single since 'Paranoid' turned into the meanest kid on the block, back in August 1970.

The analogy of changing socks comes to mind, but we won't use it here. Nonetheless, though, they exchanged the Meehan company – which had recently ousted Jim Simpson – with Don Arden. Simpson was livid, and when Osbourne took the stage months later, during a US tour, he was handed a subpoena regarding what the ex-manager believed were unsubstantial reasons leading to his dismissal. A two-year litigation battle ensued.

Still, Sabbath's main concern was making records, and although Thomas Wolfe stated it perfectly when he wrote, "You can't go home again," they gave it a whirl. "I think that [period] was a little bit of a downfall, in some ways, because we all went through a stage of having time off and wanting more time at home and taking it easier," points out Iommi. "I think that started settling in around *Sabbath Bloody Sabbath*. We came over [to Los Angeles] to do *Sabbath Bloody Sabbath* after the *Volume 4* album, which we really enjoyed. Great vibe, great atmosphere. We had great fun. We recorded that at the Record Plant. It was fantastic there. We brought over Tom Allom, who's worked on all the albums with us from that time. He was mainly the engineer, really. Patrick Meehan stuck his name down in 'production', and his ego got involved. And so, with the next album, *Sabbath Bloody Sabbath*, [we thought] we'd come back over here and try it again, recreate the same thing, 'cause it worked well on *Volume 4*. So we came back to the same house [in Bel Air, the quintessential glitzy neighbourhood] and got everything the same, except, when we went down to the Record Plant, in this room that we'd been in, they'd built this giant synthesiser in there, so it was all different.

"We were totally shocked. We didn't know what to do. And also, when we came over, nothing was working the same. Ideas weren't coming out the way they were on *Volume 4* and we really got discontented. Everybody was sitting there waiting for me to come up with something and I just couldn't think of anything. I don't even know what it was at the time. It wasn't happening for me. And if I didn't come up with anything, nobody would do anything."

It's important, at this juncture, to emphasise how many times this theme would appear in this author's conversations with the guitarist. The remaining three members admit that 99 per cent of all Sabbath songs began with an Iommi guitar lick. There is no quibbling over the fact. Again, even in a democracy, some people have more democracy than others. By default, Tony came up with the ideas. By possessing a larger creative breadpan than the others, he produced more ideas. However, whenever the guitarist would speak about this pre-production process, he was bitter that Ozzy or Geezer never came in with the grain of a song, a seed which might be fed and nurtured. And perhaps there lies in this brief observation the feeling, on Tony's part, that he had earned and deserved the right to the band's name and to carry on producing music under this banner. Indeed, he would go on to carry the name on his own.

Here are Iommi's own recollections about the making of the fifth record and the band's return to England: "It was like I was to blame, I think, because I couldn't come up with anything. So then we had a little break and decided to go into a hired castle in Wales. It was an old castle and we rehearsed in the dungeons there, and it was really creepy down there, but it had some atmosphere and it conjured up things and stuff started coming out again. I think one of the first [songs] that came out of that was 'Sabbath Bloody Sabbath'. I just started this riff and then they started up, and it worked well."

The muse this time, then, was a place, not a person or a thing. What makes Tony's anecdote so wickedly funny is that the very element which created them – call it the dark side, the Devil's kiss or the burdens of the beast – is that same unknown that scared the band so silly that they were reluctant to stay in the castle when recording sessions were over. Maybe that's why a vampire can't see his own reflection in a mirror – it might scare the bite out of him.

"The only thing was," says Tony, all six feet plus of him laughing at the memory, "we were frightening each other so much that different members of the band were driving back home instead of staying there. And it was a long way from where we lived. It was right in the middle of nowhere, this castle. It was creepy. And it did have a ghost. Ozzy and myself did see something there, one day."

Seriously?

"Seriously, yeah. I don't think that ever came out in a song, because we rehearsed in the dungeons. Ozzy and I were walking from the rehearsal room towards the armoury, where they had their weapons and stuff, and we saw this guy coming down, dressed in black. [The fifth member?] He just went into this door and I said, 'Who's that?' and we both sort of looked at each other and said, 'Who the hell was that?' Nobody else was in the castle, apart from us and the people who owned it. So we went into this room to see who it was and there was nobody else there and there was no other way out. It was creepy, really creepy. The next day, we said to the people who owned the castle, 'Look, we saw somebody here last night,' and they went, 'Oh, don't worry. He's seen a lot. He's the ghost.' *What?* It was really weird."

Aside from apparitions – organic or imagined – and not following the dictates of the prior album, this fifth record, finally liberated in November 1973, was a minor milestone of sorts. For the first time, keyboards were tossed into the stew, and this new sound taste was palatable not only to the public but to critics as well – *Sabbath Bloody Sabbath* bubbled its way to Number Four on British logs and by January of the following year was simmering at Number Eleven in the USA.

It was precisely these minor changes – the addition of strings and synths – that kept them from bogging down in their sometimes over-calculated, under-impassioned brand of brain-knocking music. To set the record perfectly straight, however, it must be noted that Tony tinkled on 'Changes' from *Volume 4*, and Geezer also plunked on a Mellotron. 'Changes' first took shape while in Los Angeles, before the return to the English castle; there was a piano at the rented house in Bel Air and, while the guitarist was plunking around on some chords, the rest of the band heard the ideas, found inspiration and turned the song, ultimately, into 'Changes' (the track on which Rick Wakeman appeared).

This chronicle has touched upon the subject several times, but it has always been Sabbath's inner sense, the unspoken voice of member number five, that told them when too much was enough and not enough was overload. Musicians freeze-frame themselves when they find their muse, apply it and apply it again and again and again. A moment lasts but for a flash, and an audience who loved the sound of those 300 guys beating on empty cigar boxes with a number two Ticonderoga soft-lead pencil on their last album now want to take the new record, comprised of ten tracks of stogie-box-pounding mantras, and set it on fire like a $12.95 Havana. Listeners have memories measured in sub-atomic time – they forget very, very quickly. If they've heard it before, they don't want to hear it again; and if they've heard it again, and it didn't sound as profound as the first time around, they'll forget it.

Sabbath knew this. Collectively, they probably had the shortest memories of any four musicians ever to tread the Earth. If they couldn't remember what they did on the record before, how could they duplicate it? 'Paranoid' kept the attention of millions of kids for three minutes plus and plunked them atop the hits hill, but nothing on *Master Of Reality*, the follow-up album, sounded like this. Of course tracks had similar textures. The same four musicians were doing the creating. Call it the fifth member, instinct, intuition or creative negation – that is, "We did that. We'll never do it as perfectly a second time, so why not try keyboards? Strings? More acoustic guitars?"

Keyboards? Why not? They called Rick Wakeman to lay down some synths and *Sabbath Bloody Sabbath* then had a new wrinkle, a new face. You have to break the old nose before you receive the new one. But it wasn't a Yes album. No one would ever mistake it for a King Crimson opus. They knew when to apply the brakes.

"*Sabbath Bloody Sabbath*, I thought, was more of a continuation from *Volume 4*," says Iommi. "I think *Volume 4* was more of a new step from *Master Of Reality*, because it took a jump, there. I think, as far as we were concerned, *Sabbath Bloody Sabbath* summed it all up, as far as what we were trying to get at that time, with the words and the songs and the way it was going. I mean, with *Sabbath Bloody Sabbath*, we could have continued and gone on and gone on and, by the time we'd finished, we'd have been getting more technical than anything. We would have been getting into using orchestras and everything else, which we didn't particularly want to do, so we ended it on *Sabbath Bloody Sabbath*, and we took a look at ourselves. And what we wanted to do was basically a rock album, [which would take shape on the follow-up, *Sabotage*]. *Sabbath Bloody Sabbath* wasn't a rock album, really."

These ensuing comments are engaging because they give voice to that muse which oftentimes inserts an idea but then leaves the critical decision "Is this piece even worth working on?" to the insertee. Being one's own editor has certainly scrambled more than one grey-matter omelette.

"We didn't feel that [*Sabbath Bloody Sabbath*] was wrong, but we felt that we didn't want to lose our identity. We didn't want to lose our own thing. We're a basic rock band, really, and we wanted to go back to our basic thing.

"*Sabotage* is nothing like the first album, but it is a rocky album and it's far better produced and better sounding than the first albums. It's more polished. Well, not polished. That's not the word, 'cause I don't say we're a polished band at all."

Polished or not, some of the sheen was beginning to come off the nails, and they were starting to crack. Near-constant touring interspliced with making records and consuming ever larger and more frequent amounts of narcotics and alcohol were beginning to pollute the process. Ward had become a virtual stumbling zombie (he'll admit to this) and there were buzzes and whispers about Ozzy's ever-growing desire to strike out on his own.

What makes all of this so difficult to comprehend is that, at this musical crossroads in their career, the band were turning out startling compositions. They had breached that gap whereby acoustic instruments, keyboards and off-kilter arrangements were all elements accepted by a record-buying assembly which, more times than not, probably went to sleep each night chanting a dozen hallelujahs to old Beelzebub itself. Black Sabbath could toss out the rare ballad – not too often, mind you – and get away with it. Their music around 1973, 1974 and 1975 still contained all of the slaughterhouse carnage bottled up in an Osbourne vocal; Iommi's playing, emanating from beneath mutilated fingertips, touched you in the way that candlewax will burn you ever so sweetly as it drips upon a naked wrist – you keep your arm/ears there without moving and then, when you think you can't take any more, you light one more match or listen to one more song; and Ward and Butler were locked at the heart, prisoners of their own crazy rhythms and afraid to let go of each other for fear that they'd never end up at the same place again and with absolutely no chance of arriving there at the same time.

But feelings as uncontrollable as the heat of the sun were starting to burn their way to the surface. Bill Ward, even as numb as he was, most of the time, could sense the fires growing in them all, and he shivered: "By the time of *Sabbath Bloody Sabbath*, I was really diminished by my narcotic use. Something happened further up. One or two of the guys started to discover it, and by that time I wasn't participating as much as I used to. But that was a great album to do, because that was when my son was born. They wouldn't let my second wife enter Great Britain* because she was an American citizen, so we were going through all of this immigration thing. We did most of the work on that album in a big castle in Wales, and I would commute to Belgium every couple of days between sessions to see my wife. I do remember when we did 'Sabbath Bloody Sabbath', because we were in this very old stone room. Oh, it sounded real good."

But not good enough to silence the flames.

---

* The band returned to the UK to complete *Sabbath Bloody Sabbath*.

"In *Sabbath Bloody Sabbath*, I don't know whether you're aware of Geezer's disgust. I don't know whether you can hear his tiredness. By this time, there's little things like, 'Bog-blast all of you,' which is just the sarcasm and the rejection going on there."

Where did these emotions come from?

"Maybe just the tiredness. Maybe some complacency from this tremendous force of energy here [pats his heart]. I think it becomes dangerous when one thinks one can change the world with music. I found it safer just to play music. Then, if someone reacts and wants to change, it works better. Sometimes power can give you the idea that you're going to change the world. The world is not going to change. It'll do its thing in its own sweet time. But I think there were some things going on in *Sabbath Bloody Sabbath*. There was some tiredness. Even the title itself provokes sarcasm, to some degree."

Complicating matters was the ever-returning though never-verified rumour of Ozzy's departure. Even the singer himself, in talking about the *Sabbath Bloody Sabbath* and *Sabotage* records right around the time of making them, paraded around like a peacock. He was genuinely happy with both records, but...

"I think the music is definitely going in a better direction," said the singer about the *Sabotage* project. "When you set out to record and write an album, you never sort of sit down and say, 'Well, this is going to go this way.' I think this last album is the best one we've ever done. I think it shocked a lot of people. It shocked the shit out of me. As far as the strings and the bagpipes, we just tried it. We said, 'Well, fuck it.' We tried anything and everything.* If it's good, it's good. Try anything once, because it's your record.

"A song like 'Fluff' on *Sabbath Bloody Sabbath*, that was an acoustic thing. I tell you, I'd really like to do a lot more mellow stuff on record, but I dig rocking on stage, you know? I get bored on stage when I'm singing a ballad. They want to hear 'Iron Man', 'Paranoid', 'War Pigs', 'Snowblind', 'Sweet Leaf' and that's it. I need a band of my own to do the mellower stuff. But I dig singing the spacey things with electronics. I dig this emptiness thing. The synthesiser gives this empty feeling of depth and distance. It's like forever. Like 'Who Are You?'. I wrote that in the kitchen while my wife was cooking some food. I had a synthesiser on the table and I was just fucking about with a tape machine and it just came out. It was the first thing I had ever written on my own. I never played instruments. I don't even know what the fuck I played. I really don't know what key or chord or what notes I played. It's just the sound. That's the best way I get it. I can make a sound which I think other people will like without getting into the musical trip, without saying, 'Oh, that's G major, F sharp,' you know? I'm not involved with all that trip. I mean, when people start talking, 'Play this in F sharp or A minor,' I don't know what the fuck they're talking about. It's just another number to me, another address."

That odd gumbo, seemingly incongruous ingredients stirred together, made Sabbath such a character study.

---

* Later, however, when Ozzy had left the band, he would cite these albums as the turning point at which the Osbourne/Iommi roads separated. He wasn't happy with the direction that the guitarist was taking, and certainly even a cursory listening to these albums outlines the sounds and types of songs that Tony would compose when working with new vocalists.

Ozzy will admit to "coming up with the occasional riff" but balances the statement with a rejoinder such as, "But I don't profess to being a musician. I can't play a piano. I only use one finger on a synthesiser. That's my fucking bag – my one-finger fucking solo. Liberace on one finger." And then there's Tony, a constant source of inspiration through which the other three funnel their ideas. Bill, as it finally appeared on his later solo material, was a prolific creator of sounds and a damned fascinating singer in his own way, as evidenced on 'It's Alright' from the 1976 album Sabbath *Technical Ecstasy*. And Geezer, beyond his brutal yet balanced four-string plucking, was ye olde poet, the wordsmith able to take oft-covered themes such as love and war and confusion and understanding and rearrange them in novel and never-before-heard statements.

"We discovered that I like the heavy stuff," sorts out the singer, "Tony likes mellow stuff, Geezer likes heavy but mellow combined and Bill writes lonely stuff, very sort of sad stuff. Combined, it must have fucking clashed. It was a weird trip to be in. I went to Tony's house one day and he'd done this thing on a piano and a Mellotron. It sounded like a fucking symphony. I said, 'Fuck, man, what's this?' He's always piddling about in the band with a synthesiser.

"I believe this was *Volume 4*. That was like the beginning of a new trip for us. *Sabbath Bloody Sabbath* was stage two. On *Volume 4*, we opened [the audience's] eyes to what we can eventually do. It's like opening another door."

Yes, the band catapulted themselves over the outer

creative wall, dog-paddled across the moat and, with the unleashed power of four brains ticking in sync, batter-rammed the final castle door. This one had been guarding the true secrets of imagination, and once the portal fell into splinters, Sabbath found themselves among a plethora of passageways, the keys to the kingdom finally in their grasp, hence the introduction of synths, strings and choir-like backing vocals. In the same fashion that Led Zeppelin sought out and discovered their own "fountain of truth" with their fourth album, in the same way that The Who upgraded themselves from mere excellence to sheer God-like status with *Who's Next*, Sabbath finally unleashed their own bullets and arrows.

Sabotage, made available in September 1975, was a beginning and an ending. Although the record wasn't their strongest, it was pungent with the aromas and flavours of that gumbo that had been five years in the cooking. 'Hole In The Sky' and 'Supertzar' were messengers of breaking the sound barrier, of things to come.

Unfortunately, the wheels were slowly running down. Drugs, burnout and the "expectations surpassed and now what do we do?" syndrome were all plagues. Recorded at Morgan Studios in England, *Sabotage*, like the title of the prior album, was a sign that something was wrong.

"We had so many problems on that album," ruminates Iommi. He knew that the band were in the midst of a swan-song and it pained him to speak about it. "We were going to break up with management [a problem that haunted the band from its inception] and we were getting sued for this and that while we were trying to record an album, and that was rather difficult. But we got through it."

Again, as pointed at earlier, Ozzy was still a 100 per cent member, but a deep gaze into his eyes revealed vistas completely foreign to the Sabbath domain. "Everybody would put their part to it," remembers Iommi. "Ozzy just worked different. While we were working something out musically, Ozzy couldn't do anything, so he would just go out and play pinball or whatever he'd want. So we put the ideas together and then he'd come back and start singing something, and then we'd say, 'Come and have a go on this,' and he'd come in and have a go. I mean, it was fine."

There were undeniable moments: 'Supertzar' utilised a mountainous guitar lick supplemented by a 50-piece choir, while 'Am I Going Insane (Radio)' was built around a Moog and another subtle furrow. Whispers aside, this latter track was to have been the title of an Osbourne solo album. Each member was presumably working on his own project, but these never materialised – at least, not on vinyl. The kernels were there, though, and internally taking shape, so the notion of splitting off and doing separate recordings was a seed planted and fertilised.

Bill Ward similarly saw this era as a challenging one, both in terms of dealing with sharks in suits and in terms of attempting to develop more completely melodic and harmonic sections. In his own words, "I wanted to take risks. I wanted to move further." On a piece such as 'Who Are You?', from the *Sabbath Bloody Sabbath* album, the drummer was confronted with a track containing pianos and keyboards and certainly not the typical amplifier-driven tune, but he loved the song and was inspired in trying to develop arrangements and parts as yet unheard by the Sabbath faithful.

"Actually, that was pretty simple. When Ozz came down to do that, he was very happy, that morning, and he got me out of bed and recorded it. It was easy for me. I mean, when I say easy, I'm not trying to sound egotistical; I just naturally knew where to put it. It was just a good feel. If I'd had my way – which I didn't quite get, 'cause it was Ozzy's song – there were some more drums that I wanted to do and tambourines. I was really supportive of him, too, 'cause it was his first song. Everything was his, 'cause we collaborated a lot, but Ozz came down with this and we worked with him on it. There's a big difference there, you know? But, God, I wanted to add so much more stuff to really enhance the track. I just had visions of monks travelling across the desert and stuff like that. Yeah, a very imaginative song."

Another track, 'Looking For Today' (*Sabbath Bloody Sabbath*), had the drummer playing rolls and fills, as opposed to a straight two-and-four bass drum with a one-and-three snare. This was Ward more as a percussionist than a drummer and goes back to his earlier comments about orchestrating phrases as half of the rhythm section. "I tried to make a bit of room for everybody else," he diagnoses his role on this particular album cut. "I don't know. With these things, it just comes. It's hard for me to pinpoint, sometimes. This stuff just comes intuitively. You just know where to put it." But when questioned about songs like 'Don't Start Too Late' and 'Solitude', Bill has a pat answer: "You know, I can't remember the track now!"

But the guitarist does. Although the band was spinning in different directions and emotions were tossed in the air and blown four different ways, he still recalls an unbridled love for their music. "We've always been serious about the music. We didn't look on it as a money thing. Even then, when we listened to the older albums, we always thought of something new we could have done on them. But when we play on stage, we still get the same feeling we had back in the early days. The albums at this time and the early albums always reflected how we felt and where we were at the time. It was always a reflection of the group as individuals, as a band."

With management changes, from Patrick Meehan to Don Arden (the father of Sharon, the woman Ozzy would eventually marry), came a label switch in England, from Vertigo to NEMS Records, while in America they remained on Warner Bros. *Sabotage* would be the album that marked the end of Sabbath Mach I. They had grown consistently as writers and performers, and this all culminated on this sixth album. In a final summation, Iommi clears the webs from obscure corners and reveals feelings for some of these songs: "Well, let's see. We've got one track called 'Hole In The Sky', which is the start of the album. That's a basic rock song. Guitars, no extra instruments, no keyboards or anything. We do try and choose certain songs to open albums – we go through the routine, the running order of them – and 'Hole In The Sky' we thought was an opener. Geezer wrote the words to that. That's sort of a universal thing. It's basically about the astral planes.

"In between that and the next song is an acoustic guitar thing called 'Don't Start (Too Late)', and the way we came about that was the engineer was a comical chap and he kept saying, 'Don't start! Don't start!' But it was too late, because we had started.

"And that leads into another song called 'Symptom Of The Universe', which is another rock number, and that changes tempo into a jazzy sort of thing, while I do an acoustic thing.

"After that, it's a song called 'Megalomania' [laughs]. It's hard to quite explain that number. Geezer wrote the words, so he's really the one to answer that. That song starts as more of a slow thing, like 'Hand Of Doom' on the album *Black Sabbath*." (The cobwebs became a little thick here – 'Hand Of Doom' is actually on *Paranoid*.) "It's sort of a slow starter and it builds up in the intro into a rock thing.

"That's the A-side. The B-side starts with... [Tony pulls out a white-label cassette and starts to laugh.] We've got all the wrong titles on here, all the joke titles, like 'Choir', 'I've Got 15 Cows' and some others. But there's 'Am I Going Insane (Radio)', which is a sort of Moog guitar groove.

"And then we've got the choir one, 'Supertzar'. In fact, I think this is before the Moog one. [It is.] "And then we've got 'The Writ', which starts with a wah-wah bass and changes tempo at the end into a different sort of thing."*

Were they pleased with *Sabotage*?

"Yeah. Well, we'd have to be," says Iommi, "otherwise it wouldn't be a test [laughs]. There's only been one album where I wasn't personally pleased, and that was *Master Of Reality*. I liked a couple of tracks on

* This is a song dealing with the band's ongoing nightmare with management, lawyers *et al*.

it, but I thought it could have been a lot better. At that time, we'd been moving around and were bushed. But, you know, we're pleased with the albums to a great extent, now, because we can produce them ourselves. Everything we want, everything we do, we know we're doing it ourselves – keyboards and all that. I mean, we could go deeply into it and really go mad [in the studio], but we'd never be able to reproduce it on stage. We can dub and dub and dub and put loads of stuff into it, but we've got no chance in heaven of playing it on stage. So the idea now is playing it on stage. We've got a keyboard player with us now. He hasn't joined the band – we don't want another member – but he helps us live. He's not known. His name is Gerry Woodruffe. He only plays on [two] numbers on stage: 'Spiral Architect', from *Sabbath Bloody Sabbath*, the one with the orchestra, where he plays Mellotron; and he plays on 'Megalomania', organ and string synthesiser. We just added him for the tours so we could get the same sound on stage."

One critically important live date during this period was the group's appearance at the California Jam in Ontario, California. Touted as an all-day affair, it presented more than a dozen bands and finally ended with Black Sabbath, Deep Purple and Emerson, Lake And Palmer, respectively. What made this show so incestuously appealing was that, in this line-up, Deep Purple included bassist/backing vocalist Glenn Hughes, the singer eventually to become a member of Sabbath and who would appear on the *Seventh Star* album (1986). Also, Ronnie Dio, although not present that afternoon, would sing in both Sabbath and Rainbow.

But Sabbath's set was an important one because they hadn't been seen by an American audience for some time and in one fell swoop their English profiles would be glimpsed by a crowd of well over 250,000, not to mention the other 20 million or so viewers who would later watch them on a television special. "That was great," gushes Iommi. "We really enjoyed it. I mean, we didn't know what was happening. We were just in England, and we didn't know whether we were playing or we weren't playing, because we'd heard reports back that it wasn't going to be very good. Nobody knew we were coming over, so we said we wouldn't go over. And then we sent our road manager over there to see what it was like. We thought it was going to be another mess up, where you'd get to a festival and find nothing organised.

"Then our road manager rang us early in the morning and said, 'Look, it's great. Everything's together.' I was in bed. I woke up half-asleep, half-awake. As far as we knew, we weren't even advertised. Nobody knew we would play. I rang everybody else, got them out of bed, and we got a quick flight over. We'd had no rehearsals for months before came over. Well, we had one rehearsal in LA for about a half-hour, and then we went on and did the show, but we just got to the stage and went in to play.

"It was Deep Purple, us and Emerson, Lake And Palmer arguing about who was going to top the bill. And then we thought it wasn't really nice, I mean, [arguing over] who was topping the bill, so we thought, 'All we want to do is go on and play.' I think it helped to introduce Sabbath to America again. But, coming over on the plane, I was thinking, 'Oh, Christ. I wonder if the amps are gonna work? We haven't had them checked out.' But I wasn't thinking, 'Am I gonna play right?'"

Tony needn't have worried about that aspect. As happenstance would have it, this writer attended that memorable show and Sabbath played like the very Furies themselves unleashed, like the Four Horsemen conducting their own Kentucky Derby. Their set coursed with adrenalin, and although there were the minor mistakes – hitting a wrong chord, crashing cymbal-wise where no accent was needed – this was a show that certainly should have made the band proud. We have to tell all of the truth here, though, and the night did belong to Deep Purple. Lead singer David Coverdale warbled like a deafening diva and Glenn Hughes' vocals were mesmerising. A flashpot was ignited and almost took off the back of Blackmore's head, but their renditions of 'Mistreated' and 'Burn' had "classic" written all over them. I also remember Sabbath that day being helicoptered onto the site prior to taking the stage and indulging in a bit of snowblinding powder, Tony bringing out a five-inch-high vial and shaking out the contents on some type of table.

Bill Ward, too, has his connection to the moment: "It was like the elite or something. I remember going on stage and I lost my air for what seemed like an eternity. Actually, it was probably only for a few seconds. What happened was, I have to count the band in, and when I count the band, so everybody gets it. But the crowd were coming forward and they were all yelling, so there was an actual vacuum in the air. You could actually feel the rush. I had no air. I'm trying to get air to scream back,

'One! Two! Three! Four!' at the band, and you *know* you've got that somewhere, but there was just so much air coming from the audience, so much energy. It was like a force field coming across the stage. It was almost like trying to walk into the wind. But then, once the band came in, we were fine. We started to rock 'n' roll."

Here, Ozzy reminisces about that eventful day: "The band said, 'We're not going to do it.' I said, 'You're crazy. We haven't been on the road for, like, three or four months. This is our only opportunity where a lot of people can see us in a short amount of time in one gig.' Millions of people could see us and realise that we were still surviving as a band. Otherwise, we'd have to go in there for another six months and play all the towns. And at the last minute they said, 'Yeah, okay.'" (This differs from Tony's version, in which he contacted the other members, but memory is a vicious beast, devouring itself and spitting out half-eaten truths and untruths.) "So, we flew straight into Los Angeles. We rehearsed. We hadn't played together for months and months and months. We got together, went straight down there, did the gig, and it was great, one of the most memorable gigs in my life in the Sabbath days. It seems like another life now, the old Sabbath days, like a dream. We had good times out of it, but we also had a lot of misery. Towards the end, we weren't the best of friends. Everyone was trying to fight everybody else, 'cause everyone didn't want to own up to themselves and say, 'It's over.'"

Ozzy knows about endings as well as anyone, and he felt that Sabbath should have expelled its last breath many records ago: "If they would just shelve that name!

This is not just me being jealous. They should have shelved the name from the word go. What have I got to be jealous for? Maybe in the future, if we all decided to do a one-off tour with the original line-up, we could go back on stage, do our own stuff again and it would have been great, but it's too late for that now.

"At first, there was a lot of resentment on both our parts. I think they hated the fact that I was doing things on my own and I hated the fact that they were carrying on the name Black Sabbath. They should have scrapped the name Sabbath and started again. They're competent, good players, and it's like [flogging] a dead horse. There are no bad feelings any more. At first there were, but not any more. I suppose, if I had been a failure, then it might have been a totally different thing, but I'm doing all right on my own."

8 Changing Horses
In The Middle Of A Dream

Maybe it was simply to bide time, or maybe they felt that
it was the appropriate time, but for whatever reason, the
band decided to assemble a compilation album, which
they titled *We Sold Our Soul For Rock 'n' Roll* (1976).
A live album would have made infinitely more sense, but
logic is a trait not usually found in the music industry.
Recorded at Criteria Studios in Florida, it was 70 minutes
(plus) of the group's signature songs up to that time:
'Paranoid', 'Iron Man', 'Black Sabbath', 'NIB' and a
dozen others.

   This record truly represented the end of Black Sabbath
Mach I. From this point on, the music would expand
and Sabbath would bring in more outside players (Gerald
Woodruffe would play an increasingly larger role) and
the music itself would take on more cinematic qualities.
Arrangements would become more studied and the actual
sound of the records would evolve into more of a
technical wash – guitars a bit more processed, vocals
greased up somewhat and an overall smoothing of edges.

   For true Black Sabbath fanatics, the first three albums
provided the songs that truly carved the band's identity.

Raw, aggravating, Devil may care, the music served no other purpose than to convey the thoughts and desires and needs of four British boys embracing the acts of rehearsing, writing and recording music in an almost religious sense. This is all they were and, more importantly, all they ever needed.

But, perhaps in an attempt to simplify matters, those first six albums were really the original footprints. Following *We Sold Our Soul For Rock 'n' Roll*, the Sad Four (as some people were now thinking of them) released *Technical Ecstasy*. It wasn't a bad album, but this 1976 disc just didn't say much. It was a sad foreboding of what was coming – and come it did. Those antsy signs that Ozzy had exhibited a couple of years earlier could now be read by the blind. That addiction to the music portrayed on those first half-dozen albums had disintegrated into a pale and weak urge. There is no finite answer here, no mathematical theory to explain their emotional malaise. All we can do is listen to their own words and try to arrange in our own minds what may have been happening. The Never Say Die tour would be their last with the original members, and it really came as no surprise to anyone.

"We were tired," whispers a whimsical Ward. The *Never Say Die* album (1978), for all intents and purposes, was the end of Black Sabbath for those screaming supporters who knew the band, essentially, from the music they created as Mach I. "I think I was tired, too. I came up with the title of *Never Say Die*. I was looking for a title for a long time, and when we were in rehearsals and we were sagging and a bit of disjointed and disillusioned, I just thought... Me and Ozzy had put a lot of work into what it would be, what we thought we could hold onto – a title, a theme, something that was gonna work, something that was powerful, that would fucking push it through. And then I started relating to my usual things about the British Air Force, stiff upper lip and all that kind of thing, and I think Ozzy made the connection to it, so I got the endorsement from him. So now we had two against two. Sometimes we had to get votes in there. So it was accepted, and it was like some motto to push us through to the other side."

These final lines in Bill's statement are interesting, inasmuch as you can feel politics creeping into the creative sweep. On the earlier albums, the music cast the deciding vote, and it was a virtually unanimous agreement all the time.

"It was getting pretty bad," continues a brutally forthright drummer. "I was getting ill all the time with my drinking. We were running all over the bloody world to make this album. We went up to Toronto, Canada. We went all over the place to try and make this record."

Ozzy, too, felt as if the blood was running backwards within his veins. Money became the motivator, and by this time the disease was rampant: "As I was the vocalist in Black Sabbath for so long, I was setting up a set way of writing. The formula I had was, I'd have a guitar riff and I'd sing over a melody line. Then we'd put some words around it and work on it. Sabbath got out of control in the studio towards the end of the days. I mean, they wouldn't let go of those few little loose ends. But I think people like to hear the guitar player make a slight mistake, so it sounds like a human being playing instead of a robot.

"The last Sabbath albums were very depressing for me. I was doing it for the sake of what we could get off the record company and just get fat on beer and put a record out. Nobody was really interested in promoting it. No one was interested in getting out there and working on the road.

"*Never Say Die* was my last album with Sabbath. I didn't finish it, either. I just did that last record and said, 'Okay,' and walked out, 'cause I couldn't stand it any more. In fact, 'Goodbye To Romance', on my first solo album [*Blizzard Of Ozz*, 1981], was just about farewell to the past, farewell to Black Sabbath."

Ozzy was temporarily replaced by ex-Fleetwood Mac and Savoy Brown vocalist Dave Walker when he exited the band. Tony tries to assemble the pieces of what would become a tremendously complex personnel puzzle: "By this time, I was booking studios and doing everything. I'd say to them, 'Would you want to do it in Miami? There's a studio there. I'll get the details.' And so, if anything was wrong, it was my fault. And then we had *Never Say Die*, and that was when the problems started setting in deeply. We were rehearsing, and then Ozzy left the band. Then we brought in Dave Walker and we wrote some songs with him. I booked a studio in Toronto, and three days before we were due to go into the studio, Ozzy wanted to come back into the band! And then we said, 'Oh, shit!' He wouldn't sing any of the stuff we'd written with the other guy, so it made it very difficult. So off we went, plodding off to Toronto with basically no songs.

It was at the height of winter, freezing cold. Why we did it, I don't know.

"We'd write in the morning so we could rehearse and then record that night. That's how bad it got. It was like being a machine. You had to write this music to record on an album. It goes down – thank you and goodnight, onto the next. It was like a conveyor belt, when we did that, and you couldn't get time to reflect on stuff and sit back and look at it – 'Is this right? Is this working properly?' That, to me, was an album that was very difficult. Particularly, it was very difficult for me to come up with the ideas and try putting them together that quick."

What were the reasons for Ozzy leaving?

"Well, maybe it was the tension. He wanted out because we were going through those stages and it was a bit detrimental. Maybe he was calling everybody's bluff. I don't know. We were all into silly games. But it was hard. I mean, we were in Toronto for something like five months. It was quite a long time, and we were getting really drugged out, doing a lot of dope. We'd go down to the sessions and have to pack up because we were too stoned. Nobody could get anything right. We were all over the place. Everybody was playing a different thing. We'd go back and sleep it off and try again the next day."

But Tony always felt confident about the players in the band and has nothing but high praise for the rhythm section that supported him for so many years: "[Ward and Butler] were brilliant. They were great as a rhythm section. Superb. We all worked so well together. Everybody knew what to do. There was no, 'Oh, what are you going to now?', 'cause everybody knew that everybody was capable of doing whatever we wanted to do."

Finally finishing this ninth album, Sabbath went on the road once again and had as openers a band called Van Halen. At this time (1978-79), the LA-based band were still relatively unknown (their first album had just been released), and Tony had no real knowledge of them or the young guitar player who bore the quartet's name: "It was their first world tour. They came with us for eight months. We had worked with a lot of bands before that, but I thought they were very good. Excellent."

With the tour ended, the band returned to Los Angeles and remained there for eleven months. Once again, they secluded themselves in the ritzy digs of Bel Air and, in a communal spirit, opted to make another album. But drugs were still bending and blurring all decisions and all circuits shut down. Ozzy claimed that he had no ideas. The band would present him with bits and pieces, but his main response, Iommi remembers, was one of "frustration". In the meantime, the label was scratching at the door, a great unfed wolf demanding its sacrifice. It wanted to hear new songs, and it had been nearly a year since its voracious appetite had last been appeased.

By this time, there had been an abundance of serious conversations regarding the very real possibility of breaking up. Bill and Geezer knew that they couldn't continue in this fashion and voiced the mutual opinion that, if a new project wasn't set in motion, they would leave. Ultimately, it came down to Ozzy. Did he desire/not desire to remain a part of the band and look towards the future?

The true emotions spilling out at this time – the

balances of power within the band and hidden agendas – have all been fuzzed up by the passage of years. Tony says that they approached Ozzy and declared, "If we don't do something, we'll bring in another vocalist." And that's what they did. At the suggestion of Sharon Arden, Osbourne's wife-to-be, they contacted Ronnie James Dio.

"At that time, I think Ozzy had come to an end," Iommi relates. "I think he just had to sort himself out a bit. We were all doing a lot of coke, a lot of everything, and I think Ozzy was getting drunk a lot at that time. We were supposed to be rehearsing and nothing was happening and it got worse. He just started coming and going. It was like, 'Rehearse today? No, we'll do it tomorrow.' That's how bad it got. We didn't do anything. It fizzled out.

"And then, when we brought Dio in, he came in with a different attitude and started singing to some of the riffs we'd got, and we thought, 'Oh, great!', because the riffs took on life. They did work. And then Geezer left for a while, because he had personal problems going on at home and he said, 'Look, I can't handle it. I've got to go home and sort my life out.'"

Although he admits openly that many of these dialogues and exchanges lie in a chamber for which he's lost the key, Bill Ward has his own take on the situation: "I was pretty gone back then, so these are tough times for me to remember. There just wasn't as much freshness. I'm not sure what was going on with Geez. I don't remember it all. Maybe it's just as well that I don't. But I knew, from a musical point of view, that Tony and I almost went back to our childhood. Things like 'Johnny

Blade' [*Never Say Die*] – the groove on that reminds me of the club days. So we knew *we* had to carry on. Tony and I, musically, we had to close ranks, and I know that I tightened up with Tony a lot.

"I think that Ozz just got pissed off. He needed some time out. The guy was in pain. This was when Jack, his father, died. When Jack died, Ozz was extremely upset, to say the least. He was a little dysfunctional, having a tough time wanting to show up and do things. I don't know if something happened there – I'm not even exactly sure what happened, to be honest with you – but *something* happened, where Ozz took it upon himself to say, 'Oh, fuck everything. I'm out of here.' So he went back to his house in Staffordshire. And then we were Ozz-less. That's when I think we were starting to look at other singers. I knew I couldn't base anything on Ozz, 'cause there ain't nobody like Ozz, so in my thinking I still thought of us as a blues/jazz/hard rock band."

This was the point at which the name Dave Walker came up, actually at Bill's suggestion. Dave rehearsed with the band and did all of the rough vocals for *Never Say Die* but, in the end, "It just wouldn't happen." The band actually appeared at a number of gigs with this line-up, including some inconsequential television gigs, but the magic wasn't there.

The four personalities who make up Black Sabbath are four of the most gregarious, open and forthright people you could ever meet. Over the years, they've always treated people with respect. Bill Ward, in particular, is a gregarious character who gets along with everyone, and for him to damage a person in any fashion is a characteristic not in his psyche. This all goes to underscore the insidious and devastating effects of drugs and drink, when a person of this make-up can be transformed into a living, breathing monster. When the band were indulging in these vices – and it was most of the time, during these waning years – they became a mean-spirited animal.

Dave Walker was a friend of Bill's and he wonders to this day how he let the singer know that his services were not needed: "I hope I was professional. I might not have been, actually. I'd get drunk and stuff. When I'm drunk, I'm gone. I'm dead. I'm fucking horrible."

So was alcohol a contributing factor in the group's demise?

"Oh, it was definitely one of the most damaging things to Black Sabbath, and not just me alone. We were destined to destroy each other. The band were very toxic. We could brush this under the couch and be cool, but let's not. Let's talk the truth and call it toxic. That's what it was."

In the in-between, Ozzy returned to finish *Never Say Die*, the subsequent tour, and then entered Ronnie Dio. Geezer had also departed and was (temporarily) replaced by Craig Gruber, a former bassist with Ritchie Blackmore's Rainbow. Actually, long-time friend Geoff Nicholls was initially recruited for four-string chores before eventually moving to keyboards, an instrument he'd never played before. In actuality, Nicholls' main instrument was guitar.

This new ensemble began to work on material, and the first piece to take shape was what would become the album's title track, 'Heaven And Hell'. Bill does recall the writing session for this song, and it was as if that fifth member had demonstrated his too-long-invisible presence: "It was about four o'clock on a Friday afternoon, at the end of a long and tedious week. Nobody had a clue what to do, so we just went, 'Fuck everything.' Ronnie was getting his bags and leaving for the day. [The band were stationed in LA.] I think it was Geezer [who had returned from England, his main reason for leaving being to spend more time with his children] who started playing *boom ba-ba boom ba-ba boom* [imitates bass guitar]. I was out by the swimming pool and I came into the living room, where the drums were, and I sat down and started playing. Then Tony came running down the stairs with a guitar in one hand – I *think* he had his underpants on – and he said, 'Hang on a minute. I've got something for that.' He plugs his amp in, and from the point that happened, it was that phenomenon again. It was still there."

'Heaven And Hell' took shape in 45 minutes. In Bill's mind, this was the last remaining residue of the original Sabbath's method of magic-making. The band then migrated south to Miami and resided at Barry Gibb's house while recording at Criteria Studios. 'Die Young' was another of the first songs assembled.

The title track and 'Neon Knights' were both carefully crafted and rockfully convincing songs. It's just that the album sounded more like a Rainbow record, which always sounded more like an Elf record, and so on and so forth.

Dio, born Ronald Padavona on 10 July 1947 in Portsmouth, New Hampshire, is an intelligent and highly copied vocalist, and when he put his own solo band together he truly left the mark of his own signature. *Heaven And Hell*, which came out in April 1980 and made it to Number Nine in the British charts, was a substantial effort for what was essentially a new band. Had Dio been the singer on the group's nine previous records, his work on *Heaven And Hell* may have marked the emergence of a new era for Sabbath, but Ozzy is a hard act to follow.

Tony attempts to explain the differences between the two vocalists: "They were totally different altogether, not only voice-wise but attitude-wise. Ozzy was a great showman and still is. He was one of the lads that you would sing along with, and we grew up together. It was a different kettle of fish altogether. We knew Ozzy and accepted Ozzy for what he was, and he knew us and accepted us for what we were.

"Then, when Dio came in, it was a very different attitude. It probably had to be a little more professional, because he came in with a different voice and with a different musical approach, [in terms of] vocals. He would sing across the riff, whereas Ozzy would probably follow the riff, particularly in 'Iron Man'. Some of those songs where he followed the riffs were great, but Ronnie came in and he had a slightly different approach, and it sparked us a bit more. He gave us another angle on writing. We were getting a little more adventurous on some of the songs on *Heaven And Hell*, and that worked great. After that, we went out and toured. It was a challenge again. We had to prove ourselves. We were going out with a new singer."

A challenge? Absolutely. Not unlike that first jump from the plane – you know that the parachute will open.

You're certain it will open. You're pretty sure it will open. Nonetheless, you must exit the aircraft. The remaining Black Sabbath trio *did* jump off the plane and fell to earth again with Captain Dio. Meanwhile, keyboardist Geoff Nicholls brought to *Heaven And Hell* an expanded vista and allowed Iommi a chance to play in a mellifluous and lyrical way, somethid he had touched upon with earlier records but which came to the fore on this one. Even so, don't think for a minute that the remaining members didn't focus on the unblemished truth that their lead singer was leaving and that they were no experts at parachute-packing: "We took the risk because we thought it was a great band," defends the guitarist about their decision to forge ahead.

Before continuing with Tony's comments, it should be brought to light that this is a choice that many bands face in a career, and there are tugs and pulls on both sides of the equation. Is it proper for a group that built itself on the backs and within the minds of a distinct and select combination of musicians to carry on if one of those persons leaves? Does it have the right, the moral or creative weight on its side, to walk ahead? What if a member dies? We could cite dozens of examples here, but some bands hit very close to home: Led Zeppelin, The Who, Traffic (flautist Chris Wood passed on some years ago). Zeppelin even went as far as to issue an authorised edict that, in honour of the death of their drummer, John Bonham, they would no longer play music together under this banner. For the most part, they've held true to that promise – there's been the one-off Zeppelin appearance and the more recent Page/Plant collaboration titled *No Quarter* (although what is sacrilege is their refusal to allow bassist/keyboardist John Paul Jones to participate – a narrow-minded option). Perhaps, then, as tragic as it sounds, a member who leaves doesn't earn the same respect as one who dies?

On the other hand, is a band not more than the sum of its parts? Was not Sabbath some creature, some breathing, salivating entity with a life beyond that of records and concerts and magazine reviews? It existed on a different plane, and for millions of Sabotees this was an experience as real as licking an ice-cream cone, as exhilarating as a first kiss, as dangerous as a cigarette. Sabbath was not – on this level, mind you – Osbourne, Ward, Iommi and Butler.

With more questions posed than answered, Tony finishes his thoughts: "We write some great stuff. Why should we just stop? We were glad when we got [Dio]. People are obviously going to say, 'No, it isn't going to be the same.' It was a risk for everybody. [Certainly Ozzy must have felt like he was treading water at the time of his exit.] And then we went out and proved ourselves and started selling out arenas."

Ozzy, meanwhile, tries to throw a candle flame on some of the shadowy emotions that he was feeling at the time: "After working with Sabbath for all those years, I forgot how to have fun – not just off stage, alone, but on stage. And when you consider that you live together in a confined area for months on end, it helps if you can have a little bit of fun and let off steam, like throw a bottle at somebody. When we were with Sabbath, we'd come off stage and go our own ways. It was like he'd go to his room, I'd go to this bar, somebody would go to a strip club. It wasn't bad, but it gets boring. Who wants to live six or eight months on the road and not talk to anyone and backstab everyone? It's an unhealthy situation to be in.

"You get married. You get stuck in your way of life. You know that you come home from work, you get your slippers put on, you get the newspaper, a cup of coffee, you watch the TV, have a few doobs and go to bed. It becomes a way of life until you say, 'Well, what's it like on the other side of the fence? I'm sick and tired of this life, but I'm frightened to jump over the fence, because once I've jumped, I ain't going to get back again. But I've got to try and salvage my life.' Which happens not only in rock 'n' roll but in life in general. We became an organisation that wasn't very organised. I didn't have the guts to say, 'I want out.'

"When I first left, I thought, 'What am I going to do? Where do I go? I've never auditioned anyone in my life.' I didn't have the first idea what to do, and at that time I never had any management. [His wife, Sharon Arden, would ultimately take on that role.] You're stuck in a big, cruel world and it's like, where do you go? I didn't know how to go about it."

Even after management was in place, the singer had to try and deal with the physical side of the situation: "At first, I was so disillusioned and so disappointed in myself, because at that time I was drinking heavily, taking a lot of chemicals to get through the day, until eventually I just said, 'This ain't no good. I've got to pack it in and live.' And the funniest thing was that, at the time, Black Sabbath was being managed by Don Arden, and I thought that the company would be angry at Sabbath, but actually it was the other way around. They gave the other guys the goodbye to keep me on, which was a great, great feeling for me. I'd never been so low in my life as that time."

Eventually, in 1980, John Michael signed with Don Arden's Jet label. In the meantime, he had located Randy Rhoads, the pivotal spoke in the wheel, and with a new guitarist in tow released *Blizzard Of Ozz*, which reached the Top Ten in England and blew to Number 21 on the other side of the Atlantic. A year later, he divorced his first wife, Thelma, and married Arden's daughter, Sharon, on 4 July 1982. She soon took the management reins and in 1984, as part of the deal, committed Ozzy to the Betty Ford Clinic, a drug/alcohol rehabilitation facility.

On 19 March 1982, a cruel and stupefying plane crash took Rhoads' life. His brief replacement was Night Ranger Stratocaster-slinger Brad Gillis, who was quickly dismissed upon the arrival of ex-Ratt man (before that group ever recorded) Jake E Lee, born Jakey Lou Williams. Jake was Randy's antithesis – he disdained the whammy bar and opted for Fender-styled instruments, as opposed to Rhoads' choices of Gibson Les Pauls (during his Quiet Riot days) and later the Jackson Flying V-inspired pieces.*

Although Tony never opted for the silver straw, the sterling spaghetti – the whammy bar – Ozzy had built a large part of his sound around Randy's tremolo-arm calisthenics and the singer made quick note of the fact that Jake was a man without a bar: "The first thing Ozzy

---

* Grover Jackson, later a creative director for Washburn and Rickenbacker, was pivotal in assisting Randy in the development of his guitar. This creation and sound would sway the fingers of legion players.

said was, 'Do you know how to play a guitar with a whang bar on it?'" mentions Lee. "I said, 'Of course. Anybody can play a guitar with a whang bar, but I don't like it.' And he said, 'Well, why don't you think about using one? Because I don't think you can play some of these songs without one.' And I said, 'I can. I'll show you.' And, after rehearsal, he said, 'Yeah, fine. It sounds like you've got one. I don't care.' He was almost under the impression that a modern guitarist cannot play without a bar. You're limiting your vocabulary that way. I proved him wrong, I hope."

His main string squeeze was a *circa* 1974 Fender Stratocaster featuring Gotoh tuners, brass bridge and Gibson frets. The rosewood fretboard sat atop a maple neck. The instrument boasted a pair of single-coil DiMarzio SDS-1 pick-ups slanted opposite the normal position in order for the pole pieces beneath the bass strings to lie closer to the bridge, thus producing more bite and less mush.

Jake must have swayed the singer about bars and guitars, because he remained with the singer for two albums, *Bark At The Moon* (December 1983) and *The Ultimate Sin* (February 1986), but he was not persuasive enough to become a permanent member because the screamer dived into the personnel pool yet again and came up with merman Zakk Wylde. A New Jersey product, Zach Adams, born 14 January 1966, was a Les Paul snob who approached the whammy arm like a wild dog – he never ventured close. Zakk's wild-finger-vibrato-produced sweeps shook you like a careening freight train and at the same time moved you along sweetly like a horse-and-buggy ride. There was a profundity to his playing that most of his peers lacked, and Ozzy sensed this instantly.

Ozzy's sense about guitarists was uncommonly remarkable. His ability to search out and procure that sole, unique and transcendent element has played a monumental part in his durability and ongoing success. It's as if he has donned the persona of a modern-day John Mayall or Alexis Korner, bandleaders from an earlier era with an uncanny knack for scouting out rookies and turning them into legends. (Mayall played alongside Eric Clapton, Peter Green and Mick Taylor, and Alexis also developed a stable of young and blossoming prospects.)

So Zakk brought his Les Paul to the Osbourne team in August 1988 and remains with him to this day. He appeared on several records: *No Rest For The Wicked* (October 1988), *Just Say Ozzy* (March 1990, live), *No More Tears* (October 1991), *Live & Loud* (June 1993, another live-r) and, most recently, *Ozzmosis* (October 1995).

Lynyrd Skynyrd, The Allman Brothers Band, The Eagles and even Mountain are all hitching posts on Wylde's frontier, inspirationally speaking, and this becomes yet another pat on the screecher's tattooed back. Ozzy heard these Southern-fried licks, took this bell-bottomed boy and plucked him from that terrain to become a wrangler in his own werewolf-riding, bat-shooting rodeo. The singer was able to see beyond what was happening in the here and now and to perceive what might happen five minutes from now. This is a truly wondrous gift we speak about here, and although nay-sayers may think, "Hell, Ozzy is a star and could pick any lamer with a guitar to be in his band," they are the conceptions of the brain-dead. Ozzy was masterful in his selections and he deserves the acknowledgment. If Zakk did attempt to toss in a Dickie Betts country bend, Ozzy would retort, "What the fuck does that mean? You're kidding, aren't you?" The guitarist would save these twangs for his own short-lived band, Pride And Glory, for which he abandoned the singer but ultimately returned. To this day, Zakk balances a solo career between his own Black Label Society band and his high-visibility sideman gig.

By the late '80s, Ozzy had kicked his addictions and retired to his Buckinghamshire mansion with manager/ wife Sharon and three children. In this new frame of mind, he well understood Zakk's desire to work on his own Pride And Glory project so and put out the welcome mat for Joe Holmes as Wylde's tour replacement. Holmes, a resident of Los Angeles, bridges the gap, in a sense, between Zakk and Jake. He's a Fender molester, raping older Stratocasters (1971-74) and inserting them in 1973 100-watt Marshall heads modified by Jose Arredondo, the now-deceased amp wizard originally known for his tinkering on Edward Van Halen's gear. He's a bar-bender of a serious nature, and yet he finds the more dirge-like approach of bands such as Alice In Chains an intriguing one. So in Holmes you find a mixture of the modern flash and the alternative bash, Ozzy once again twisting the tiger's tail without being bitten. "I think that's one thing I bring, that grunge," says Holmes, "because I'm really into all of that. I think I can really bring a different side. While I was growing up, it was always Ozzy, and a lot of these newer bands have all been influenced by him. Those two *Blizzard Of Ozz* albums were a big part of me, when I was growing up, and here I am playing a lot of it."

Coincidentally, when Joe was about 16 or 17, he took lessons from Rhoads, and a lot of the material he now covers in a live show will call up the response, "Gosh, he showed me that pattern." Whether Ozzy knew or even sensed this connection between the two is superfluous. Somehow, someday, he felt it and was Osbourned yet once again.

While Ozzy may have been experiencing a renaissance, Engineer Bill was being derailed. Not only were his wheels not on the tracks; he couldn't even find the train. And it was a crazy train indeed. His drinking had reached unmanageable proportions, and with the comings and goings of band members his tolerance level reached its limit. He did manage European and English tours in support of *Heaven And Hell*, but finally, during the American leg, there was little left but to give up the ghost or die.

"I was sinking very, very quickly. I was on a drunk, an unbelievable drunk. I was drunk, like, 24 hours a day, so when I went on stage, the stage wasn't as bright. It was dying. I felt like I was dying inside. So the live show seemed so bare. Ron [Dio] was out there doing his thing and I just went, 'It's gone, it's gone, it's gone,' and I had to pull out. I couldn't handle it.

"I had a friendship with Ronnie, but musically he just wasn't for me. It wasn't where I wanted to be. Ronnie's lyrics, I almost felt, had a pretentiousness, like he had actually tried to conceive what Black Sabbath was and then perform that. I'm not saying that Ronnie did that; I just felt that. But in our friendship, we were fine. I like Ronnie.

"What happened was that the phenomenon of the bottle became more important than anything else in my life. I was out of control, so I was now in the grasp of King Alcohol. And, in spite of whether I wanted to talk to Tony or Geezer or sort out any of the problems, it was beyond all that. I was in the grip of a progressive illness that was killing me. I had to go with the alcohol and I had to let it take me to wherever it would take me before I could finally bottom out."

Bill does have brief memories of Tony approaching him with Blackmore's *Rainbow Rising* album and inquiring of him what he thought about the singer. This was back in 1978, during the *Never Say Die* sessions. Whether the guitarist was innocently playing a record or intentionally planting the first seeds that would sprout a new singer, Ward is unsure. This was the first time that the drummer had ever heard Dio sing, and he candidly came forth with, "Yeah, nice singer. Cool." For Ward, however, there was never the slightest notion that his guitarist might be playing this record for him in preparation of changing vocalists.

Time-machining ourselves two years forward to 1980, Bill Ward left the band in that year during what would have been a show in Minneapolis, Minnesota. The writing on the wall was now flashing neon and a change was inevitable. And his name was Vinnie Appice.

Before we address this slap in the face, however (Bill was never told about this replacement; surely he knew it, but when he showed up one day and there was someone else sitting on the drum stool, it must have been the final cork in the bottle), we should examine the association between drummer and new singer. Bill was a close, close friend of Ozzy. Perhaps brother is a better word. So, with the arrival of Ronnie James Dio, he must have begun an even steeper southerly spiral into the bottle. When those parts of our lives are removed – a buddy moving away, losing a job, finding your girlfriend skin-friendly with another, those parts that represent our solidarity, our stepping stones – then life loses all colour. "Me and Ozz were buddies. We were the team. And when this happened, it was like, 'Holy shit! Give us a break. What the fuck is going on, guys?"

It's unfair to cast Dio as the man in the black hat. While highly opinionated, he is the ultimate pro and was brought in to do a job. So Bill had to try and make sense of this nightmare that was light years ahead of "Who's gonna play drums in Black Sabbath?"

As if this locomotive, by now, doesn't have a bumblebee's clue about which direction to head in, toss in the reality that Ronnie Dio sincerely admired Bill Ward and has nothing but lofty praise for him.

Interior-wise, Bill Ward is receiving input of conflicting data and emotions. Alcohol has essentially wiped out all rational thought. He knows that he cannot go on with the band but is cut to the core when newcomer Vinnie Appice arrives. And, although he's been a lifelong ally of Ozzy, he finds in Dio another supporter and compadre. There is only one way in which to try and unravel this paradox and only one person to do it: the fifth man. Allow this author a couple of pages to expand literary licence. This invisible entity – never seen, but felt as clearly as rain falling upon the head – will conduct an interview with Ronnie Dio. Presumably, since he/she/it is some sort of cosmic or spiritual being, this special journalist possesses insights beyond the ken of any mortal pen-pusher and certainly an intuition far outdistancing this author.

So the next voice you hear is Astral Author Number Five. Quickly, as background fodder and before this all-seeing, all-knowing presence changes its mind, let it be mentioned that the time-frame here is *circa* 1983. Dio has departed Sabbath and assembled his own band. While this is a purely fictitious exchange, responses are based on fact and, in some places, chronicled data.

NUMBER FIVE: What was it like working with this Black Sabbath band, Mr RJ Dio?

DIO: For two of the four years I was in Sabbath, I had a solo deal. I had the deal under the condition that I wouldn't step on Sabbath's toes, that the first commitment would be to the band. I did all the things I had to do to make this band successful again, and nobody can say I didn't. They can shout all the abuse they want at me.

NUMBER FIVE: Did they have reason to slam you?

DIO: The feelings are bitter because I did everything I possibly could to care about them as people – the band, their reputation. After all, Black Sabbath weren't my band; they started it off, so all I tried to do was prolong their careers and make Black Sabbath a name respected by other musicians, for a change. Before I was in the band, they were a dead issue.* When I got in the band, they became alive again, because they had some intelligent input. And now they can go back to being stupid again. I don't care whether they're successful or not successful. It makes no difference to me.

I don't mean to sound so bitter about things, but I've seen so many things in the press said by Tony and Geezer. [After hours of interviews with the band, this author can say that not once was the Dio name denigrated in any fashion.] I should tell you the way I feel. I certainly have the right.

They're going to be in the '60s for the rest of their lives. When we were in the '80s, they still wanted to be in the '60s.

NUMBER FIVE: It's common knowledge that you sang with Ritchie Blackmore's Rainbow, another band often compared to Sabbath and oftentimes maligned as residing in the past. Both groups had major-league guitarists. Any correlation here?

DIO: It was more difficult with Tony than it was with Ritchie, because Ritchie knew his instrument so well. [In another coincidence, engineer Martin

---

* On the contrary, the previous album, *Never Say Die*, charted at Number Twelve in England and the two predecessors, *Sabotage* and *Sabbath Bloody Sabbath*, carved respective niches at Numbers Seven and Four. Perhaps the singer's interpretation of the band's status was a minimalist view.

Birch worked on all related Sabbath and Rainbow albums.] He played up to his own limitations and he doesn't step beyond that. He doesn't want to be a jazzer. I think Tony wants to be Joe Pass or something. When Ritchie played through an amp, he could play through anything that came in the room and he always sounded exactly like Ritchie, because he knew what to do with it. Tony would try every amp made under the sun.

Tony is a real basic player. He's probably one of the best chord players, whereas, if Ritchie was doing a backing track, he'd just play on the E string. But it served its purpose. He wanted more space than Tony did.

NUMBER FIVE: Do you alter your approach in any way when working with such disparate bands as Sabbath and Rainbow?

DIO: When it comes time for doing a vocal, nobody would tell me what to do. Nobody. Because they're not as good as me. So I do what I want to do. I think it's always been my impression stamped on the bands I work with, rather than them making me something else, because I always sound like me. [This brings us back to a point from several pages ago, which made mention that Rainbow albums sound like Elf records and that Sabbath bore the same vocalisms as Rainbow and so on.]

NUMBER FIVE: What about your interaction with Bill?

DIO: Ozzy wasn't a very big contributing member of the band. All the lyrics were done by Geezer, and Bill sang once in a while [on 'It's Alright', from the 1976 album *Technical Ecstasy*]. He thought his contribution was to bounce up and down on stage and look like Benny Hill. He claimed to be a great performer? It must have been Stevie Wonder and Ray Charles watching him on MTV, because he looks like a fat blob to me. He puts a mic on a stand and walks around and looks dazed. But I can see what mental trip Tony must have put Ozzy through.

And, of course, Tony being the strong figure in the band has Geezer so afraid Tony will leave him that he grabs onto his tail like an elephant. [The great irony here, if you haven't already figured it out for yourself, is that Geezer did leave, Ozzy did leave and Bill became a horrible casualty, but one now resurrected.]

NUMBER FIVE: You claim to have been such good friends with these Astonians. So what happened?

DIO: I did like Tony for almost all the time we were together, and the other guys, but I don't like him now. I don't like him a bit. I don't like his attitude. I don't like his lies. Just because of the ill way I feel I was treated by him. I gave everything I possibly could to them. Sure, I did some of it for myself – I'm not stupid – but I'm the one who had to sing 'Iron Man', not them. They may have had to play it, but I'm the one who had to get up there and sound like a fool doing it. Ozzy would even bring a dwarf on stage and call him Ronnie.

NUMBER FIVE: Bottom line, RJD, is what did you think of the records you made with these apparently horrible men?

DIO: *Heaven And Hell* and *Mob Rules* were good records. I think that, if you compare the two, you'll find better songs on *Mob Rules*. [Ward had left the band by this recording and had been replaced by Appice, the younger brother of Carmine and someone who would play a key part in Dio's just-around-the-corner solo career.] But still, you can hear the discontent on *Mob Rules*, the searching. It was like, "Why are you doing this one? Why don't we do 'Iron Man Part II' or *Children Of The Grave: The Film*? Let's go back to the '60s again." On the live album [*Live Evil*, 1983], the songs are good but I haven't heard the live album. I refuse to listen to it because there are too many bad comments about it. If you look at the credits on the album, the vocals and drums are listed off to the side – another thing that shows exactly what they are.

When we did the albums, the names were supposed to be in alphabetical order: Butler, Dio, Iommi. My stage name is Ronnie James Dio, so the credits are listed, "Tony Iommi, guitars; Geezer Butler, bass." What happened to the alphabetical order? And then it says, "Special thanks to Geoff

Nicholls, keyboards." Is that what you call what he used to play? I can't believe it. The man was totally inept. He was a good guitar player [his first instrument, as we noted some pages ago]. The credits read, "Geoff Nicholls, keyboards; Vinnie Appice, drums."

Why should it be that way? Open it up and see how many pictures there are of Tony and how many pictures of me and Vinnie. They can say anything they want, it's a better album than [*Speak Of The Devil*, Ozzy's live album released in November 1982]. At least there's not a harmoniser on every song. He should get Eventide or somebody to sponsor his tour.*

This exchange complete, acrimony and feelings of betrayal running rampant, the reality that remains is the three albums processed and produced with Ronnie James Dio. *Heaven And Hell* (April 1980), *Mob Rules* (November 1981) and the live one, *Live Evil* (January 1983), represent the Sabbath band Mach III. Mach I consisted of the first half-dozen records, Mach II was earmarked by the compilation *We Sold Our Soul For Rock 'n' Roll* and the subsequent albums while Mach III might be dubbed "the Dio years".

For reasons that are difficult to pinpoint exactly, this particular expedition had parachute malfunction written all over it. You just knew, sooner than later, that the huge umbrella hovering above you was going to tear, get

---

* Sabbath's live album was due to be released in August 1982 but didn't see the light of day until January 1983. Ozzy's record, in the meantime, came out in November 1982 and made the release of the band's album a couple of months later seem particularly inappropriate.

snarled on a tall building or be pecked to pieces by the ever-present vultures. Ronnie Dio is a solo artist, and within the political and emotional workings of a band he would always develop internecine relationships – that is, both sides lose. No winners. This is not a criticism of the singer, by any means – some of us are generals and some of us are grunts, and Ronnie James Dio is Patton, Lee and MacArthur all rolled into one. Five stars.

Maybe it was because he wasn't a native Astonian. Maybe it was the already-twisted conditions of the other band members. Maybe it was because he wasn't Ozzy Osbourne. The chances are that all three notions contributed.

Drummer Ward has singularly heart-rending feelings about this space in time, that moment when he realised a metamorphosis was taking place and that the object being newly created had none of the qualities of that which sired it. Although they still carried on with Black Sabbath, this was not a name that he gave any credence: "I did the *Heaven And Hell* record with Ronnie, but I was in a pretty numbed-out state. I lied to Ozz. [Long pause, intake of breath.] Ozzy knows about this. We've talked about it. I went along with a lie. It felt horrible, really uncomfortable, going behind Ozzy's back, because we'd always been up front with each other. We built trust over the years. We had family. When you go through what we've gone through – the gigs, the years of touring and everything else – you get to know everybody pretty good, and I know that Tony felt disillusioned a little bit with Ozzy. And I'm not trying to put this on Tony. I've spoken to him about this, too.

"I lied to Tony in the sense of saying, 'Yeah, I'm interested in working with another singer,' when I really wasn't. That's when my lie began. Also, my drinking accelerated at that point, too, 'cause I was trying to kill the lie. There was talk about introducing another singer, and I'd heard Ronnie's voice and I thought Ronnie was a very, very good singer. I like Ronnie. He's a friend of mine, okay? I asked him [to join] as well. And after that, I felt like hell. There was no way out for me, at the time. I felt that I had really done some wrong, with Ozz and our relationship. I also felt that I was wrong towards Tony, because I had lied.

"Deep within me, I honestly couldn't see Ronnie Dio singing Black Sabbath. That's the truth of it. And it wasn't long after Ronnie came in that I could see Geezer slowly withdraw. [Even Dio felt this discontent during the *Mob Rules* sessions.] Ronnie is a very good musician. Ronnie is quite capable of writing his own lyrics, so the framework that we had was no longer in place.

"I don't remember recording *Heaven And Hell*. In fact, I listen to it today and I don't remember that I recorded it at all. People have told me that I did, but I don't remember that I was on the session. And when we went on the tour, about halfway through the American leg, I just simply couldn't do it. We lied to the public, or I lied to the public. We used the cop-out that I was grieving about my mother, which was actually true. But what was really going on was that booze had become more important than the band. What was really going on was that I was in real disarray over the loss of Ozz and I didn't know how to deal with the loss, and so I went into oblivion. It was two or three years later that I began to really know what had happened."

Hindsight, handgun of the imbecile and short-sighted, has since told Bill that these Dio-period works were really just bunches of solo work stitched together under a Sabbath cover. Plainly speaking, Tony was starting to drift towards a slicker and more defined sound, Geezer was "over here doing something" and the bubbling was beginning.

Tony's choice of musicians – Dio, Nicholls and, later, Appice, Cozy Powell and Bobby Rondinelli – was an indicator: "He was moving towards drummers, for God's sake. I'm not a fucking drummer."

So, in carrying on with Ward's idea, Iommi was attempting to change the sound of the band. But it wasn't completely gelling. Hence, the records began to adopt more individual characteristics than a group timbre. Bill felt that his guitar partner could have approached them and attempted to explain what he was hearing. Ward believes that solo records may have provided the answers. He cites The Rolling Stones and their longevity and attributes that to Jagger and Richards *et al* venturing off on their own and divesting themselves of non-Stones material. Had Ozzy and Tony and Bill and Geezer left the Sabbath confines to construct their own personal sound systems, he reasons that this hiatus may have been enough to sustain them. But then, hindsight is a high-calibre notion that sometimes backfires.

Bill has approached Tony with this theory, but the guitarist disagrees. Dio was summoned and Ward, in essence, was given the boot. Ward feels as if he was a bad limb amputated to save the rest of the body. Please keep in mind that these remaining three Birminghamites were soldiers in a single trench, willing to take bullets for each other. A bar stool – take away one leg and the entire chair collapses. A triangle – take away one of the lines and the remaining two have no form whatsoever. These were close and dear friends, rallying against all outside forces in order to keep the band safe and intact. When Tony sent him packing, it was like the shout was heard around the world.

"I couldn't hang with it, and the guys didn't talk to me, so they booted me from my drum chair. I wasn't told about that, and I was pretty fucking pissed about that. I knew that they'd have to bring a drummer in to work the gigs if they wanted to save them. Then save the gigs. But I've been with the band for years and years and years, since we were kids. And Vinnie was playing and it was, like, what the *fuck?* It hurt a lot."

Vinnie Appice, hired gun, provides us with verbal bullets: "They didn't know if Bill was coming back. He just left and they had to cancel a bunch of gigs. So I met the band and it was temporary for the first month, and then they realised, 'Well, this is working out really good. Bill's not coming back, anyway. You're in the band.' We rehearsed about two or three times, and the first gig was Aloha Stadium in Hawaii. 20,000 people. The *Heaven And Hell* record was already out, and Bill was on that, but they said there might be a record to do. And then I did the *Mob Rules* record with Dio. You know what those sessions were like? You booked it for two o'clock and the band wouldn't show up until seven. But we got through it and people started accepting the band with me and Ronnie."

This was followed by the *Live Evil* album, and if

sessions had been unorganized for *Mob Rules* and tempers barely restrained, this record truly represented the last nail in the coffin. "*Live Evil* was the band really starting to break up. They had differences – personal, financial, a lot of managers involved. We did the shows and came back to the Record Plant to mix and I'd be there but Tony and Geezer wouldn't be. I was disappointed. It was a great band. I loved playing with the guys. And then Ronnie said, 'Look, I'm going to put a band together. Want to do it with me?' And I said, 'Fuck, yeah.'"

Our old friend/nemesis hindsight would stick his pointy little snout into Bill's brainpan years after turning sober. It was then, he understood, that the parties left onshore – Tony and Geezer – were hurt by Bill's excesses as well. They had walked through fire together, these three pyromaniacs, and on the other side one of them was trying to douse the flames with alcohol. They felt the burn, and since Ward's sobriety he doesn't know "how on Earth they were able to tolerate me". And when Ozzy is thrown into the cocktail, Ward's delegated drinking amigo, it's almost impossible to see how Iommi and Butler put up with the pair's pink-elephant antics for so long.

Wasn't it one of those cerebral types who once said that an individual's character is truly revealed in times of major chaos? In any case, looking at Bill, one can see the fragility, anger and bewilderment lying just below the surface. All of these sensations were percolating and coagulating, and when you toss in the always-lethal ingredient of alcohol, the issue remaining is about as nutritious as a plateful of plutonium.

Ozzy, on the other side, was defiant in his stand. He

had quit several times earlier (by his own admission), and although he too was made unbalanced by beer and blow, he was dealing from a position of power: "We were fucked up heavily on drugs and alcohol, taking a lot of coke and booze. Tony Iommi met Ronnie James Dio and I knew in my heart that I wasn't into what Sabbath was doing. I had left before and rejoined a couple of times, and through all this I knew my heart wasn't into Black Sabbath, and Sabbath wasn't into what I was doing. At the end, they fired me."

Fired?

"They asked me a couple of times before, but at the end of the day they broke down and fired me, because my heart wasn't into what it was about. I can remember on one occasion they were all listening to these other bands and I said, 'This is bullshit. How come the bands that we once influenced are now influencing us? Don't you think we have a problem here?' Nobody could understand what I was talking about.

"We would do anything. We were just a fucking junk yard. When you take coke, you spend the night talking a lot of bullshit. You think you sound so fucking great. You sit in a room all night long, sniffing this fucking powder, talking lots of crap. I mean, we solved all the problems in the world, we worked it all out, but we never did shit about it. It's just talking bullshit in the bathroom. And it wasn't just them. I was involved as well. I did my fair share. It wasn't them or me. It was just like any relationship. Just because you've been with a certain girl or guy, you start to feel trapped when your heart is no longer in the relationship, but the loyalty to the relationship can be just as powerful as the love. You have to let go. [A listen to the lyrics of 'Goodbye To Romance' illustrates precisely what Ozzy is saying here.] My father died, I got booted out of Sabbath, my first wife divorced me, my new band got off the ground and then Randy got killed. It was like one, two, three, four – just like that. For all of the success I've had, it's been a very rock 'n' roll career – it rocks and it rolls, but I get back up and start again. One thing I pride myself on is that, once one door closes, I force open another door and I always keep on going forward. I've got a new band now with Joe Holmes on guitar, who was a student of Randy Rhoads."

And what did Ozzy think of Sabbath post-Osbourne?

"To be perfectly honest – and I'm not trying to say anything against them – I didn't think it remotely resembled Black Sabbath at all. I think it resembled more Ritchie Blackmore's Rainbow than it did Sabbath, with the voice. It's like, if I suddenly joined Ritchie Blackmore, Ritchie Blackmore would sound like Black Sabbath, because of the voice. I mean, you don't go down the road saying, 'That's a great riff, it's a great drum sound or cymbal sound.' You go down singing the song. It's like if I was to join the Frank Sinatra band – it wouldn't sound like Frank Sinatra, because the voice is what you listen to."

What you have here, then, is a remarkable character study. On the one hand you have Ozzy raging against the wind, battling his own monsters and familial tragedies and, like a great phoenix, vowing to arise once again from the ashes. Meanwhile, on the other hand, there is Bill, a victim of his own excess, a near-fatality almost joining his friends and kindred drummer spirits in heaven. His ascension would take years, but he would finally re-emerge with his own projects, *Ward I*, *When The Bough Breaks* and, more recently, *Beyond Aston*. The great paradox here is that he was the first one through the tunnel, the first one sober, and thus he was able to look back on his friends and pray for their recoveries as well.

9 Sod The Rules

Vinnie Appice, Carmine's younger brother (don't ask me how to pronounce Vinnie's last name; I've known Carmine for over 20 years and I still don't know, so just take a guess) was brought in as replacement drummer for Ward. To understand Vinnie's connection here, we have to drift back to 1978, when he was playing in a trio called Axis with guitarist Danny Johnson and bassist Jay Davies. Although the band were signed to RCA (there was one release), they were suffering from management problems, and when Vinnie received a phone call from Sharon Osbourne informing him that Ozzy was assembling a new band, he shifted his attention there.

Prior to working with Axis, Appice had spent time with Rick Derringer – appearing with Danny Johnson on the ex-McCoys' albums *Derringer* (August 1976), *Sweet Evil* (March 1977) and *Derringer Live* (August 1977) – and Ozzy knew his work. He ultimately turned down the Osbourne invitation, however (this would have been the Randy Rhoads band), and, by coincidence or intent, Black Sabbath tour manager Paul Clark phoned him two months later. Clark told him that the band sought a drummer and that he and Tony would be in Hollywood.

Vinnie landed the gig and was informed that it may be a temporary situation, since Bill was going through "some problems and stuff" and may or may not return. In the end, the original Sab did not come back and, following two or three rehearsals, the new skin doctor found himself performing before 20,000 people at the Aloha Stadium in Hawaii.

If we can make the comparison, and we will, Appice's approach to a kit is much more along the lines of John Bonham. He has impeccable technique, flawless timing and an arsenal of fills and flams and paradiddles. Ward was the opposite – he, like Ringo Starr, brought to the music a much simpler and less detail-orientated style which relied more on orchestrated parts than it did on elaborate bass/snare routines and dazzling cymbal work.

By this stage, *Heaven And Hell* had already been completed and Vinnie came in during the middle of this tour. The band eventually re-entered studios to begin *Mob Rules*, which was recorded at John Lennon's old house in Ascot, England, where the Beatle – shot dead on 8 December 1980 in New York City – had composed 'Imagine'. The first song on tape was the title track, which was later used in the animated film *Heavy Metal*. Recorded by Deep Purple's producer Martin Birch, this album would represent Vinnie and Ronnie's final studio record with the band. In 1982, the *Live Evil* sessions came out.

The live album really represented more of a stopgap measure than anything else. It's extraordinary to realise that the original Sabbath quartet never recorded outside the studio (although NEMS Records did compile *Live At Last*, a live recording assembled without the blessing of any Sabbath member) while here a second-generation line-up produces one. Many of the band's performances in Japan, New Zealand, Australia, Europe, England and America had been put on tape, and the idea of constructing an album of material already recorded certainly appealed to a band whose infrastructure was quickly vanishing.

There was no touring to support this album, and Ronnie and Vinnie jumped ship in order to begin work on Dio's own solo career. Ten years later, however, the pair were back to provide drums and vocals on the *Dehumanizer* album. Here's how Vinnie tells it: "I was playing with a band called World War III. We'd just finished a tour, came home, and we were having some off time and I ran into Ronnie somewhere. I hadn't seen him since I left Dio in 1990. He said, 'We're going back to England. Cozy [Powell]'s not working out.' A couple of weeks later, I got a call saying, 'Well, would you be interested in doing it? Cozy fell off a horse and broke his pelvis.' I said, 'Shit, yeah.' So I flew off to England and me and Ronnie got a house and lived there. That's where we rehearsed and wrote all the shit, and we recorded in Wales. But it was cool, because now it was like we were more grown up, mature, and everybody got along really good. It was really good, for a while."

A while?

"We did the record and then the tour started. We went to South America. None of us had ever been there, and we just did great down there. Then we did the whole tour – Europe, the States, Canada. We were doing really well, and then I guess people realised why they broke up ten years before, and that's what happened. It just got crazy."

The drummer cites management intrusions, business taking the place of the music and just generally "too much money changing hands". He was happy with the record, however, although the cover – depicting the Grim Reaper doing his deal with a none-too-happy victim – didn't appeal to him. Once again, he baled out with singer Dio to record the *Strange Highways* album.

Let us drop back, one more time, to ten years back. By no means was Tony immune to the dissolving bonds within the group. He was, in fact, terrified by the prospect of bringing in a new drummer: "Right after *Mob Rules*, we moved to California to live because, halfway through *Heaven And Hell*, Bill Ward left because he had problems with Ronnie – he disagreed with him over some things – and so we brought in Vinnie Appice. For me, I really was nervous because, after what we'd built for so many years, I was frightened to bring in another drummer. The first gig we did with him, it was an open-air show in Hawaii and I was shitting myself. I kept saying to him, 'You sure you're gonna be all right? You know how to do that?' I must have driven him mad.

"And then things started deteriorating a little bit. I think attitudes started changing. Ronnie probably wanted more say in things, I suppose, and then Geezer would get upset about him and then a little bit of rot set in. *Live Evil* is when it all fell apart. We had done that again at the Record Plant. We recorded different shows on tour and we mixed it in California. That's when we started having serious problems. We broke up at that point, in the middle of the album. [Ronnie] wanted to do more of his own thing and the engineer we were using at the time in the studio didn't know what to do, because Ronnie was telling him one thing and we were telling him another, and he really got frustrated and was freaking more and more. At the end of the day, we just said, 'That's it. The band is over.'"

Vocalist Dave Donato filled in on some live dates, but then ex-Deep Purple vocalist Ian Gillan was brought in and became the mouthpiece for September 1983's album *Born Again.** Even Ian himself admitted that he wasn't the right type of singer for Black Sabbath, but he did like the material.

Perhaps even more remarkable than Gillan replacing Dio was the return of Bill. He had sobered up for six months, but during the making of *Born Again* (a prophetically unfulfilled title) he brought his lips once again to liquor. His memories of this period haunt him still, because he knows that he was given a second chance – an opportunity few have – and destroyed it: "I left the band after doing *Born Again* with Ian Gillan. I left with shame because I got drunk. I felt terrible."

Although it sounded like a Deep Purple album, *Born Again* lifted itself to Number Four in the British charts. The band undertook yet another tour and, in the face of Ward's relapse, enlisted ex-Move/Electric Light Orchestra drummer and Birmingham friend Bev Bevan. This congregation headlined the Reading Festival in Berkshire just prior to Gillan's exodus back to a reforming Deep Purple.

---

* Here's Dio's reaction to Gillan replacing him in Sabbath: "Not only is it beyond my comprehension how he will possibly sing any of the songs they'll force him to do, such as 'Iron Man' and 'Paranoid', but I'll be real, real pleased if he's in the band, because he'll have to replace me this time. [Laughs] Now he's the one who's going to have to suffer with those idiots, not me."

Member changes for the next seven records would happen on virtually every release. Although the group continued to produce some thunderous music, under the always-watchful wand of Iommi, they lost much of their credibility on these later records. These final chapters will address themselves to this sorry, falling spiral.

10 And Then There Was One

Following Gillan's return to the home pastures of Deep Purple, there was talk about a reunion of original members, although this never got past the talking stage. But then, on 13 July 1985, the one and only Black Sabbath appeared at the Live Aid concert in Philadelphia, Pennsylvania. The event, co-ordinated by Bob Geldof, also marked the reunions of The Who, the surviving members of Led Zeppelin (there is no shortage of painful memories in a life) and Neil Young with Crosby, Stills And Nash. There was also much-rumoured talk about a Beatles reunion with Julian Lennon sitting in for his father, although this never materialised.

What did materialise was Ozzy Osbourne and Bill Ward, who had spent the previous months doing little more than lying in bed. For him, the performance was memorable, in ways contrary to what one might believe: "I'm not sure who called me or how I got the call. It might have been Sharon [Osbourne]. Usually, when I don't know what's going on at all, it's been traditional that Ozzy will usually call me and clue me in, and Sharon has been kind enough in the past to at least give me some insights as to what might be happening in my life that I don't know about. I was only sober about a year, 14 or 15 months. Remember, I had come out of a holocaust of hospitals. I hadn't any kind of knowledge of being in the music scene any more.

"I tried to fool around with a couple of bands locally [in Los Angeles], but it was all a washout. It didn't work. Part of [doing Live Aid] was trying to make up for me walking out on the band in 1983, after doing *Born Again* with Ian Gillan. I went back in 1984 to try and right the wrongs, but I just could not hang with the band at all.

"So when I was about 14 or 15 months sober, this thing called Live Aid shows up, and the only thing I could think of was, 'I've never flown sober,' or, 'I've only flown a couple of times sober.' So immediately, I've got a threat. I don't even known if I can make the gig, 'cause I'm thinking, 'Oh, my God, will I need to have a drink on the plane to cover up the fear of being out?' I'm already faced with hundreds of demons. That's what Live Aid was to me, and I had to learn how to go on stage and be relaxed. The only way that I could learn to do that was to know that the cameraman would do the cameraman's job, Tony would do his job, Ozzy would do his job and the crowd would do their job. I broke it all down. In the end, there was only me, and I thought, 'What am I gonna do? Oh, I get it. I do my job.'

"Live Aid was a blast, except that I was unbelievably out of shape. I was very ill. I was about 40 or 50 pounds overweight. I hadn't played drums since God knows when. It was a tough gig to play when you haven't played drums in a while. We did 'Paranoid', 'Children Of The Grave' and 'War Pigs'. I didn't know these guys, either. They were all pretty happening and my life was the life of poverty. I was in a very quiet part of my life at that time. Tony was still very active, and Geezer. These guys were out there and busy – managers, diamond rings and money. My life was not like that at all. It was totally the opposite.

"Live Aid was nice to do, though. It felt good. What I felt good about was that I was able to fly there and fly back without taking a drink and I was able to get on stage without taking a drink and I was able to play in front of 200 million people [the event was televised] without taking a drink. That, to me, was the most important thing. My life was at stake, and I wanted to show up because I knew it was important."

Bill went on to sober up completely and, in 1990, came out with his first solo project, *Ward I*, *When The Bough Breaks* and, more recently, his third solo record, *Beyond Aston*.

In the meantime, Tony Iommi went back to the boards with an entirely new group of players, bringing in vocalist Glenn Hughes (formerly with Zephyr and Deep Purple), drummer Eric Singer (later with Kiss) and New York-born bassist Dave Spitz. Geezer had finally had his share and left.

We shift back to Iommi, who puts this whole era in perspective: "Ian [Gillan] was one of my best friends. Getting him in the band was done on paper, basically. At the time, we went to a couple of rehearsals and Ian was trying to save his voice. He was having problems and he was going to have an operation, which he never did. Eventually, we put some ideas down, but we didn't exactly know what he was going to sing until we got in the studio. But that album, *Born Again*, should have been under a different name, really, with him singing – you know, Gillan, Iommi, Butler and whatever. I've always been a Purple fan, though. I liked them as much as I did Zeppelin.

"That's when Bill Ward came back into the band. Bill had stopped drinking for six months. Then we started recording the album and Bill started drinking again, so of course he has to go in for AA, and it was all obliterated. So we'd done a tour with that album and we brought Bev Bevan in."

The idea for the next album, ultimately coined *Seventh Star: Black Sabbath Featuring Tony Iommi*, was to be the guitarist's solo record. This record, the band's 14th (including the compilation effort), truly marked Mach III. Again, the title hinted at perhaps confusion, a conflict of interests, but by anyone's account there was a low rumble heard by everyone in the camp. The fact that on the previous record, *Born Again*, Tony didn't even want to call the project by a band name hinted strongly of what might follow: "The *Seventh Star* album is when I wanted to do the solo album. Geoff and myself wrote some songs and worked on the album. It was going to be different. The reason was that we were going to use different vocalists on the album, guest vocalists, but it was so difficult getting it together and getting releases from their record companies. Then Glenn Hughes came along and sang on one of the tracks, and so we decided to use him on the whole album. Then the management company wanted to take it as a Sabbath album, and so did the record company. You don't have a lot of choice, really, 'cause if they don't want to release it, what do you do? Their compromise was *Black Sabbath Featuring Tony Iommi*, which opened a can of worms, really, because I think that, if we could have done it as a solo album, it would have been accepted a lot more."

Glenn Hughes, a vocalist of supernatural abilities (producer Andy Johns remembers working with him on the *Hughes/Thrall* record with Pat Thrall and said that his singing technique was as effortless as that of anyone he'd ever worked with), stamped *Seventh Star* with his own bluesy interpretations of the rock genre.

Hughes, hanging from another one of those incestuous strands upon which the rock 'n' roll web is designed, actually first crossed paths with the band back in 1970. At that time, Zephyr, Glenn's band, had released their first album, *Medusa*, right around the time of Sabbath's *Paranoid*. Another Birmingham rebel, he remembers playing at Mother's in Erdington and seeing Tony and Geezer in the Trapeze audience. Later, in 1971, Trapeze and Sabbath duetted at the Top Rank Ballroom.

Years would pass before their paths crossed again at the California Jam in Ontario, California, in 1974. At that time, Glenn befriended Ozzy and Tony but became particularly close with the singer. This was the time when Sabbath manager Patrick Meehan didn't seem to be working out, and Osbourne spent nights talking to Glenn about the problems. However, it turned out that they met before the Jam, many years prior: "Ozzy lived in Staffordshire, where I was born, with his first wife, Thelma, on a farm, and they invited me to come over, so I went over a few times. In fact, I was going to buy a car from him, a Jaguar. I pulled into the driveway and, as I was pulling in, he was pulling the car out and he smashed it into another one of his cars, which I thought was hilarious."

Calling Ozzy "a character" (in a very good-natured and positive fashion) and describing Tony as being "shy at first", Glenn does have strong memories of the time he spent with the band during those Cal Jam days. The two singers spent quite a bit of time together that year, hanging out at the Beverly Wilshire Hotel. Subsequently, Hughes often spoke with the other Sabbath members – all Midlands lads, remember. "Salt of the earth" is how he describes citizens of the area.

During the late '70s, he spent some time with Tony and then, in 1981, was a regular amigo of Ozzy. At that time, Glenn was managed by Sharon Osbourne while the singer was working with Gary Moore and spent many hours at Sharon's house, where Ozzy was living at the time. They spoke of many things, even of putting a band together: "Going back to '77, when Ozzy had left Sabbath for the first time, he wanted me to form a group with him, and I had to decline because I'm a singer and Ozzy's a singer and it really wouldn't have worked. I thought we were too good friends to form a group together."

Slipping ahead to June 1985, Hughes then received a phone call from Iommi explaining that he was assembling a solo album to contain three different vocalists: Hughes, Rob Halford and Ronnie Dio. Rounding out the ensemble was Dave Spitz (bass), Eric Singer (drums) and Geoff Nicholls (keyboards), and the project was to be produced by Jeff Glixman. The tapings were to take place at Cherokee Studios in Hollywood in July 1985. "Two songs were composed swiftly, 'No Stranger To Love' and 'Danger Zone', and it became apparent to Tony and the rest of the guys that I was doing a good job. But you must remember that this was a Tony Iommi solo project. It wasn't Black Sabbath. The idea of being in Black Sabbath didn't appeal to me whatsoever. Glenn Hughes singing in Black Sabbath is like James Brown singing in Metallica. It wasn't gonna work."

Those first two tracks were non-Sabbath-oriented material, and on the face of things Hughes was impressed. After completing these tracks, Tony questioned Glenn about completing the entire album, but mixed emotions coursed through the singer's veins: "I must state this, and I want you to print this. In the '80s, I was trying to get away from the heavy metal tag. Before Deep Purple and Sabbath, I was in Trapeze and I was a very funk/hard-rock/soulful group singer. I wanted to get away from the stereotype heavy metal image I had. So, after Purple, I really wasn't interested in anything metal or dark."

The album was recorded under the Tony Iommi name and Glenn was cited as guest vocalist. Although initial sessions went smoothly, there were creases in the armour. Tony was suffering the misery of a divorce (and began spending time with, and became engaged to, Lita Ford), and on 24 August 1985 Operation Central moved to Atlanta, Georgia, to finish recording. The date has attached itself to Glenn's cranium because, on the following day, he met Christine, a lady with whom he'd spend the next ten years. She became a focus for him, and this is evident on the album – his singing, always on a marvellously high plain, has purpose and posture.

But the great monkey wrench that oftentimes loosens the bolts of brilliance and creativity arrived in the person of Don Arden. The album had been mastered and mixed and the artwork was ready when Don Arden, in cahoots with Warner Bros, "thought the album should be titled *Black Sabbath Featuring Tony Iommi*, which I wasn't really too happy with." The ex-Purple was then asked if he would like to tour with the band.

Glenn did have a "nice time" making the record. Another almost-victim of drugs and alcohol, he was indulging at the time (although he, too, is long since sober), but in the studio he was never high when he sang, even though there was pot and coke and waterfalls of alcohol on tap. The album completed, he was requested to become part of the touring band. On this, he didn't balk: "I didn't really want to do it. In fact, I didn't want to do it at all."

The question people probably want answered is, what was the difference between working in Purple and Sabbath?

"Ritchie Blackmore, bless him, is an incredibly talented guy who has a very hard time expressing himself to another human being. He's without love. He's a pretty evil cat. He's never really happy unless things are going his way, and if I had a really good night in Purple, like at Cal Jam, he'd make a point of saying, 'You know, you can't have too many more nights like that.' He's notorious for pulling the rug from under you.

"A funny story. Two years ago, I was working with my group in Oslo and Purple were in town and my band were playing a gig after Purple. A Purple fan ran into Ritchie in the lobby and he said, 'Oh, are you going to see Glenn after?' and Ritchie said, 'Glenn who?'

"But I found Tony very quiet, very shy. I think Tony is a very, very underrated writer. We all know about his guitar playing, but he's a great writer."

In January 1986, the group represented on the *Seventh Star* album were rehearsing at Alley Studios in North Hollywood, California. Before Glenn turned down the option to tour, he did work with the band for a period. In the back of his mind, though, was that nagging notion that, the harder he tried to break away from that "heavy metal, God-singer guy" image, the more strongly he was being sucked in. Most of the material he would have to sing was originally a vehicle for either Ozzy or Ronnie. In attempting to learn the material, though, he was able to formulate a stronger vision of just exactly what it was these two singers brought to Sabbath: "It wasn't so hard, singing the Dio stuff, but it was fucking really, really hard singing Ozzy Osbourne songs, because nobody sounds like Ozzy. I've got a lot of character to my voice and a lot of depth and soul and Ozzy, bless him, is a very monotonous singer. But it works for Ozzy Osbourne. You name anybody who tries to sound like him and you can't do it. [Hence, possibly, the ever-waning popularity of Sabbath, post-Osbourne.] And for Glenn Hughes to sing 'War Pigs' is an absolute crime. If you pointed a gun at me, you couldn't make me sing that song again. In fact, one night I forgot the bloody words to it in Detroit and the crowd went crazy.

"The band rehearsed for six weeks, until the end of

February, five days a week, five or six hours a night, and my voice was fuckin' rocking. It was kickin' ass. Tasco were doing the sound for me, and I loved those guys. The monitors were great. Everything was wonderful. Tony, in the back of his mind, always had doubts about me being the singer for Sabbath. I think we both knew it wasn't going to work, but Tony – bless him – is a great guy and he wanted the best for me and for Sabbath. Remember, the band was Tony's baby then and still is.

"The best I could be at the time wasn't as good as Tony wanted me to be. I just wasn't into the project. I was into the Tony Iommi project, but I wasn't into the Black Sabbath moniker."

Following six weeks of straight rehearsals, there were a few days of more refined dress rehearsals for the press. These events took place at the Lucille Ball Studios, the old Desilu facility. Following these production shows, Glenn and friends went to the Cat and Fiddle to unwind and production manager John Downing, an old friend of Glenn's since Downing worked with The Move, came along. Later that evening, after consuming some alcohol, the singer became a bit "agitated" and the production manager attempted to intervene on a conversation that Hughes was having: "[John] started getting very heavy with me and I pushed him and he hit me, and this is important: he hit me so hard in the face with his fist that he splintered the socket [below the eye] and it went into my nose on the right side. This is four days before the fucking first gig. I have a shiner and the whole band is in stitches. They think it's hilarious. I said to Don Arden, 'Who in hell is going to hit the lead singer in a group the day they go on tour?' So he hit me and he never did apologise for that."

As an outcome of the blow, blood was now dripping into the singer's throat, which he was constantly coughing up. Approximately a week later, *circa* 21 March, 1986, the band were set to go on tour. Cleveland, the site of this kick-off date, was a disaster. Glenn couldn't sing. Halfway through this first show, he knew that his days were numbered.

Surreptitiously, Tony and Arden had been arranging to locate another singer for the tour, following this Cleveland date, because they knew that Hughes was temporary, at best. Glenn subsequently met Ray Gillen, his replacement, when the band were rehearsing with Ray during soundchecks during the afternoon. "Yes, I was introduced to my replacement, Ray Gillen, and yes, I was very pissed off. I stormed down to Tony's and Geoff's room and Beast's [Spitz's] room and I banged on their doors and said, 'Would somebody please come the fuck out and tell me what's going on?' And nobody told me. To this day, nobody ever did tell me."

Glenn, the next in line to leave the band, had his vacancy filled in the studio by Tony Martin, a singer Tony used on *Eternal Idol* (1987), *Headless Cross* (1989), *Cross Purposes* (1994) and the *Forbidden* album (1995).

On *Eternal Idol*, Tony also called upon drummers Cozy Powell and former member Bev Bevan to fill in on drums and bassist Bob Daisley to assist Spitz on bass chores.

Meanwhile, Neil Murray made an appearance on the *TYR* record (1990) and *Forbidden*. Like most of the musicians enlisted by Tony, there is a history involved here. Neil was with the Japanese band Vow Wow for two albums, when they opened for Doro, the solo artist featuring drummer Bobby Rondinelli (who would later appear on *Cross Purposes*). In 1988, Neil had actually been approached to join Tony, "but at that point things were looking good for Vow Wow, so I didn't show much interest."

By spring 1989, Cozy Powell had brought energy and a sense of direction to the band. This culminated in the promising *Headless Cross* collection, with studio bassist Laurence Cottle handling four-string duties. Geezer had expressed some interest in returning (he eventually shows his chops on *Dehumanizer* and *Cross Purposes*), but he kept vacillating. Cozy, under the impression that Murray was committed long term to Vow Wow, called him nonetheless, and in March 1989 Neil met with Tony Iommi and Tony Martin at a London rock club.

Neil and Cozy went way back (here's that inbred affair again) to the early '70s, when Neil befriended Clive Chaman, bassist with The Jeff Beck Group, the band that Powell was playing with at the time. Clive assisted Neil in landing gigs, one with a band called Hanson. This band broke up (the leader sent to jail) and, after recording one album with them and performing some dates in US clubs, Neil returned to England and played with Cozy Powell's Hammer, an outfit consisting of Bernie Marsden on guitar, Don Airey on keyboards and Frank Aiello on vocals.

This band, too, fell apart, and Neil, along with Airey, joined Colosseum II with Jon Hiseman and Gary Moore. After Colosseum II, Neil did the fusion thing with the band National Health and soon received a call from Marsden to join Whitesnake. Soon he received the summons to join Black Sabbath, and since he had been working with Cozy in various ensembles, he found that "It was easy to make the material sound powerful. Cozy [was] a very forceful and committed player, and I [tried] to complement that by duplicating his drum fills where possible, although in the *Headless Cross/TYR* period he had a lot more say in the musical direction of the songs than I did, so the bass tended to be more in the background than I would have liked."

After a fairly unsuccessful US tour in June 1989, this band covered the UK, Europe, Japan and Russia before recording *TYR* during the first half of 1990. By this time, Geezer had expressed an interest in rejoining, and during a performance at the Hammersmith Odeon he actually came on stage for the song 'Black Sabbath'. Again, that twin-headed monster of management and record company was breathing fire, and additional personnel problems led to the return of Dio, as well as Geezer. Dio revisited his old haunts on the *Dio* album with his solo bandmate, Vinnie Appice. "Some months later, it was a good excuse to replace Cozy with Vinnie Appice when Cozy was badly injured by a horse collapsing [and dying] on him," remembers Murray. "Cozy and myself worked with Brian May until the end of '93, but work was thin until October 1994, when Tony asked us if we wanted to play on the next Sabbath album. At first, he still intended to use Bobby Rondinelli, who he was very happy with, but the management persuaded him to revert to the *TYR* line-up, which, in retrospect, had worked well.

"Looking back now, I think that Tony would have been happier to have kept Bobby on, as Cozy tended to want to return to the power structure within the band, with himself and Tony making most of the decisions, and the musical style that the band had been pursuing five years earlier. Given the undistinguished showing of the *Forbidden* album (1995), maybe some of Cozy's opinions were justified. But it was obvious, on the US tour in July 1995, that he wasn't enjoying playing and was unhappy with too many other aspects of the band to make it worth continuing with the band.

"Given that some people will always compare any version of the band unfavourably to the original line-up, I think the versions of the band that I have been part of have been pretty strong, musically. Certainly, I feel that we performed the material from the '70s very convincingly on the most recent tours. However, I will concede that the musical taste of myself, Cozy, Bobby and Geoff Nicholls – who has quite a lot of influence on the musical direction of the band – was not particularly for the incredibly heavy death and doom metal that Sabbath was the originator of. It has to be said that Tony Martin's voice and lyrics have a major effect on how the band are perceived, and although he does have an excellent voice, he lacks the personality and spooky quality of Ozzy and the power and charisma of Ronnie Dio."

Neil is an extraordinarily honest individual and a mindful and dedicated player. These last Black Sabbath records do have their moments, but it is difficult to take them as seriously as earlier works. Again, let's put the onus on Iommi to suss this out: "After the *Seventh Star* record, we did *Eternal Idol* in England and Monserrat, in the West Indies. The West Indies was for us away from everything. It allowed Geoff and myself to sit down in the house, where we had keyboards set up, and start putting ideas together. Then we brought Bob Daisley in to play bass, once we'd got the ideas together. Ray Gillen [who subsequently died of AIDS] was originally involved in this. This was difficult, because it was, like, the fifth record, where I was the only original member. I mean, in the early days, when we started this band, it was all guitar based, and if I didn't come up with a riff at that time, the band wouldn't have been as it was. Anyway, we brought in Tony Martin and finished recordings at Morgan Studios in England.

"Then there was *Headless Cross*. That was a completely new start again. I had to rethink the whole thing and decide that we needed to build up some credibility again. We brought Cozy into the line-up and a session guy, Laurence Cottle. He's a brilliant jazz player. Superb. We recorded that album in a very cheap studio in England, which was great. That was what I wanted to do.

"Then there was the *TYR* album with Cozy, and we brought Neil Murray in. In fact, Neil came in on the *Headless Cross* tour. We did very well in Europe with those two albums.

"After that was *Dehumanizer*. Then that line-up was broken up and the band members split. I do regret that in a lot of ways. I broke it up. We were at a good point then. Geezer's wife at that time phoned me about whether I'd talk to Geezer, and would we talk about having

Ronnie back? So when Geezer and I talked about it, we said, 'Yeah.' I don't know why, really. I mean, there's the financial aspect on one side, but that wasn't it. I seemed to think that maybe we could recapture something we had. So we reformed that line-up, and Cozy and Ronnie just didn't get on. They argued. But then we got Vinnie and eventually we put [*Dehumanizer*] together, which took a long time. It was just hard work. We took too long on it, and I didn't like the idea of that. I wanted to just go in and do it.

"That album cost us a million dollars, which is bloody ridiculous. And after that, we broke up while we were on tour. Then we got together with Bobby Rondinelli and Tony Martin and did *Cross Purposes* [1994]."

Conspicuous by his absence, bassist Butler would also leave the fold following the *Cross Purposes* album. His enthusiasm, like that of Ozzy before him, had grown dangerously thin, and the band that had once meant so much to him was now a burden too heavy to shoulder: "*Cross Purposes* wasn't even supposed to be a Sabbath album. I wouldn't have even done it under the pretence of Sabbath. That was the time when the original band were talking about getting back together for a reunion tour [1994, right around the time of the Costa Mesa get-together – see Author's Outsight]. Tony and myself just went in with a couple of people, did an album while the reunion tour was supposedly going on. It was like an Iommi/Butler project album.

"In fact, a lot of the stuff I wrote for my original solo project ended up on the *Dehumanizer* album, when

Ronnie came back into the band. Then I finally got totally disillusioned with the last Sabbath album that I was on and I much preferred the stuff that I was writing to the stuff that Sabbath were doing, so it was time to leave.

"I'm really sensitive about my music, and I don't like people telling me to change this or change that or interfere with it. Ozzy always kept telling me to do the solo thing. He said that there's no feeling in the world like it, because you've got total control and you don't have to deal with everybody else's egos. I'd been scared to go in and see what it was gonna come out like, but I just wanted to have fun again, and I love doing my own stuff. The enthusiasm is back now, and it's been so long since I've had it that I'd forgotten about it. I don't have to sell millions of albums to keep everybody happy; I'm just doing it purely for the music, instead of the fame or money."

Why so many personnel changes?

"If you've got an attitude, there's no point in carrying on. That's why we replaced different people, because [attitude] just brings everybody else down. If somebody in the band is going, 'Oh, I don't want to do that, I don't want to do this, I don't want to travel because it's too early in the day,' it's all problems, and you don't need that. You've just got to get on and do it, enjoy it, you know?"

On *Forbidden*, Tony brought in Body Count guitarist Ernie C as producer, and the result is a satisfying one. The sound, while still dominated by Iommi's left-handed guitar, has a more modern sheen, more in your face. Tony had heard the Ice T records and was impressed by the production (handled by Ernie C). An A&R liaison communicated with Sabbath's manager. The Sabbath camp said, "We're interested in having Ernie produce the Black Sabbath record." The guitarist – also a left-hander – thought it was a joke.

Finally, though, Ernie C took the helm, working in studios in England, Wales and Liverpool. He tried to bring a more contemporary flair to the sessions: "I just wanted to record the record the way the band sounded. They wanted to move forward, too. They just needed some energy. They don't need a producer. Anybody can produce them. It's simple. I mean, Body Count is all I know, so I basically took the Body Count principle of recording and we did it over there, and it worked. They basically record the same way we do, so it wasn't difficult. I'd work with them again, because it was really pleasant – except for the mixing, because the record company stepped in and they started saying all kinds of excess stuff. First of all, we mixed the record and it sounded like Alice In Chains or Nirvana. It was real dry. It didn't sound like Sabbath. But they were so scared that it didn't sound like Sabbath they wanted us to redo it. We sent this mix to the record company and they were going, 'It doesn't sound like Sabbath. It sounds like some new group.' It was dry – the guitars were in your face and the vocals were in your face – so they wanted us to wetten it up a bit. So they remixed it, and it was sounding [like going] back to the '80s, and we were going, 'Records don't sound like that now.'

"The thing that happened that made everything cool was, when I went back over to England to mix, Brian May came down, and he said, 'It sounds good. It sounds really vibrant and energetic and it sounds like you're playing like you did 20 years ago.' It was cool because Brian came in, Tony's really good friend, and said he liked it. But the record company still wanted a big-sounding Sabbath thing. They wanted more of the same.

"But then, later, a record company guy came down and, on a track called 'Can't Get Close Enough', he said it sounded like Soundgarden, and that got Tony upset. He was flipping."

11 Bodies, Necks, Skins And Tongues – The Implements Of Construction

TONY IOMMI

Tony's first aspiration was to be a drummer, but after realising the expense, he turned to the accordion. Yes, the accordion. However, after a short period of shouldering this unwieldy piece of gear, he turned to guitar. His first instrument was a Watkins, which he ran through a small-tubed Watkins amplifier.

His first substantial piece was a Fender Stratocaster (year unknown) plugged into two Marshall 4x12 cabinets powered by two 50-watt heads. One evening, during a Sabbath performance in Germany, a pick-up on the Strat kept malfunctioning and he turned to a standby Gibson SG that he always kept for emergencies. The Gibson neck and fretboard had more appeal for him than the Fender did, and he also found that he could bend notes more easily on the SG. He never reverted back to Fender-styled instruments and, in the ensuing years, developed his own singularly styled SG spin-offs. The southpaw later snatched up a variety of Gibsons, including a three-pick-up Les Paul sporting the SG configuration (similar to Eric Clapton's psychedelic-painted SG), a newer-model SG and a junior, which Leslie West presented to him as a gift.

Because he was a left-handed player, the instruments had to be modified. Looking back in hindsight, he now realises that his problem might have been solved by simply plucking a normal guitar for righties and turning it upside down. Instead, he opted for left-handed guitars, which were pretty rare in the early '70s.

On that original double-horned Gibson, Tony replaced the stock pick-ups with specially-built low-feedback units. The factory pick-ups produced a palatable tone offset by uncontrollable feedback and screeching. Swapping these with replacements allowed him more control over the chalkboard squeals. Playing at deafening volumes – as he normally did – still gave birth to these unwanted cries, but in time he was able to keep his strings as quiet as a hummingbird's whistle.

The volume came from his ever-increasing arsenal of amplifiers. As the band became more well known, Tony's reputation did not go unnoticed by gear manufacturers. Laney approached him with "an attractive advertising arrangement", resulting in an amplification set-up consisting of six 4x12 Laney cabinets fed by four 100-watt heads. Everything was channelled via Y-cords plugged into the normal outputs (Laney tops feature normal and treble feeds) of the quartet of brains. As if this wasn't enough, during this experimental stage, a Rangemaster treble unit was also linked to provide additional output. (They were reworked with extra tubes and boosters.)

As previously stated, Tony removed himself from the tips of his left-hand digits in a freak metalworking accident, and he was forced to fashion plastic thimble-like prosthetic cups to protect the tips. This mishap necessitated a drastic change in playing technique (covered in Chapter 5), while a further accommodation required the changing of string groupings. In those days, Tony combined Ernie Ball lights for the high E and B strings and Piccato light gauges for the remaining quartet. Even this far back, he was tuning down to D (instead of the customary E-standard tuning) to get more depth. This was another reason for employing light wires – bending heavier sets would "rip my bloody fingers apart".

Assisting Tony in this adjustment was luthier John Birch, the man who replaced the pick-ups in the SG. Now a stalwart Gibson guy, the Italian was intrigued with the prospect of a 24-fret guitar. He approached Gibson, but their interest was less than overwhelming. Necessity, that great mother of creation, poked him in the ribs. He knew that, if he wanted a fretboard 24 spaces long, no one would build it unless he did. He contacted Birch, who built a piece with two dozen frets. Next, they developed special pick-ups, and this association is one which continues to this day. John may have been the only one interested in designing this instrument because he was…well…a bit out of tune with the rest of us. He later poisoned his wife to death and went to jail.

Nonetheless, Tony used John Birch-designed instruments. On *Forbidden*, he used several guitars, including the Iommi Artist from Eggle, a sort of modified SG-configured piece with a Brazilian mahogany headstock and ebony fretboard. On several tracks, he whipped on a new Les Paul Custom. There isn't much acoustic work within the Iommi sound family, although he does own a Gibson J-50 and various Guilds. (Close friend Brian May opts for these, and Tony was influenced by the Queen guitarist's kingly tones.) He used a Guild twelve-string belonging to producer Ernie C, and since the Body Count member is also a leftist, he was not only able to provide Tony with guitars but had a deeper understanding of how he developed parts and essentially how he approached his instrument.

Tony, never one to hang himself on the rack, punched, pressed and pulled minimal knobs on this last record. Again, Ernie brought in his custom-made box and made suggestions for its use. The rack included an Eventide H3000, Jimmy Dunlop wah, two Furman Power Conditioners, a Boss tuner, two 1200 wireless units, a Jimmy Dunlop rack-mounted wah, a GCX Ground Controller, a Mesa amp switcher, a Guitar Silencer, a Phase-90 and a Univibe.

Still, Iommi opted for more of a straight-in sound, although he did grease things here and there, utilising his Laneys. Ernie C turned him on to Mesa Boogies and the Rectifier, which Tony quite liked and made use of for rhythm tracks. Cabinets were mainly 4x12 Laneys miked up with various standard units, such as Shure SM57s.

The beauty of Tony's playing is, and always has been, in its simplicity. For the most part, it's a John Birch six-string through a Laney 100-watt stack with double cabs. The first Sabbath records sported the tall one with Gibson SGs, and in fact the two original SGs – one red, one black – were stolen. (The former came back to him about seven months later. He insists that it was cursed.) On *Paranoid*, he switched to a white Les Paul SG and a black Les Paul, dubbed "Black Beauty". He can't forget his brief flirtation with Strats in those early days, though, and indeed he was using one when he appeared in The Rolling Stones' *Rock 'n' Roll Circus* film.

This film was a milestone for the young player: "That was definitely an event, that was. All those people are dead now – you know, John Lennon. I didn't know any of them at the time. I was like a fish out of water. But it was great, because I got to know all of them in that three weeks of filming. It was fabulous, because we all became really good friends. For me, it was a wondrous time to meet everybody at the same time. It was The Who, Clapton, Lennon, just everybody who's anybody. The Stones. It was good for me but frightening, at that time, 'cause I was out on a limb. I hadn't a clue what I was supposed to be doing, not the faintest idea. Suddenly, I was pushed into a role and I had to dance around and we were becoming actors and playing as well."

GEEZER BUTLER

Geezer is another meat-and-potatoes player, in terms of gear selection. His amp choice, as it has been for years and how it appears on his *Plastic Planet* record, is Ampeg – the SVTs, as well as Trace Elliot. For a while, Ampeg went out of business and he switched to Crown power amps, in combo with an Alembic pre-amp. He has also noodled with Marshall pre-amps. Live, he courses through Marshall cabinets with ElectroVoice speakers.

Essentially, he has always used Fender Precision basses, but on his record, as well as the *Ozzmosis* album, he fingered a Vigier. He also uses this latter model for live work. Pretty basic. He recounts the people who prompted him to switch from guitar (he started off as a rhythm strummer) to bass: "Without a doubt, Jack Bruce from Cream was my idol. I never even thought about bass guitar until I went to see Cream. And I used to love McCartney, but for different reasons. And then I saw Jack Bruce and something just went *boiiing!* It was like, 'That's what I want to do,' and it just completely turned me on to what bass should do, 'cause he had a totally different style to anybody else, bending all the notes and everything. I was playing rhythm guitar at the time in a band that I had with Ozzy, Rare Breed, and when me and Ozzy left, nobody wanted rhythm guitar any more. And I saw Cream and I thought, 'That's what I've gotta do.' But I couldn't afford a bass at the time, so I took two strings off my guitar and played bass on the bloody horrible old guitar I had. In fact, when we got together for the first Sabbath line-up, I was still using the guitar strung down. I just couldn't afford anything. And then I borrowed a bass from a friend, the bass player in Rare Breed, when we were still called Earth, and I had to borrow it to do gigs. That was the first time I ever played bass."

BILL WARD

Bill began his career with Sabbath on a Rodgers kit but had already switched to Ludwig on the band's first two albums. He made another swap to Slingerland, a Buddy Rich-inspired detour, which he described as being "an excellent, beautiful kit". When the band began making money, he admits, "I had all kinds of drums. I mismatched all my drums." When the group travelled to America, he headed straight for Manny's Music in New York, perhaps the most prestigious and famous music haunt in the entire country, and bought out every six-inch metal snare that he could lay his hands on. Up to that point, he hadn't known that such a creature existed, since everything he'd previously pounded on was either a four-inch wood or metal drum. He remembers buying ten or 15 of these rare prizes. They were all Ludwigs, since he found in them a thicker, bigger and richer sound and felt that they were easier to play on stage.

His original bass drum measured 24 inches, on the first two albums, but he subsequently increased this drum to a 26-inch Goliath, which was part of the Buddy Rich Slingerland set. He even kicked on a 28-inch floor kettledrum for a while. "They had a bit more sound to them." he adds. "Yeah, I used 28-inch bass drums. [Note: *drums* is plural. By the third or fourth album, he was using double basses, the situation that caused so much consternation to his single-bass-drum-playing friend John Bonham.] Although, looking back, a good sound can be gotten from a 20-inch bass drum, too. One of my rigs that I use today is a 20-inch Gretsch jazz kit. It gets an incredible sound. But back then, I needed to pass air for the drums on stage, and the guys would always come down to hear bass-drum cues, and so we moved up to big drums.

"In the beginning, it was horrible, trying to compete with Tony and Geezer on stage. I had to kick ass on drums, 'cause every time they'd turn up [the volume], I'd turn up, or I'd try to. There were no microphones. In those days, miking a drum kit was unheard of."

Although Bill's memories tend to drift in and out, like a radio station not fully tuned in, he's fairly certain that, by *Volume 4*, he had switched to a double bass kit. This opened up the band's sound immeasurably (and make for one jealous Zeppelinite), and while Bill will be the first to tell you that he was never a very good drummer, his manoeuvres on this fourth and subsequent recordings are really worth listening to.

Funnily enough, on *When The Bough Breaks*, he isn't even playing drums. Ronnie Ciago is his stickman. Why wouldn't a drummer play drums on his own record? Bill's response is intriguing: "The drummer man in me doesn't want to play any more; it wants to teach, to pass on information. There are a lot of good drummers out there. I listen for the soul. It's very important to me that I have musicians who will support the creativity. Musicians are basically my fingers. I know how to make records. All the time, I like to think that I'm learning, about myself and what I did wrong on the last album. Actually, we don't spend a lot of time on drum sounds. I used to spend a lot of time on drum sounds. Also, studios are quite modern now, but I use combinations of live overhead mics and at least three mics on the bass drum, and we use these shotgun mics for positioning.

"Now, the drumming man inside me wants to play and will be saved to play with Black Sabbath. The drumming man inside me is now there to teach and pass on to children and anyone who's interested in percussion. That's what I like to do. That's where he lies now. But the songwriter is very much alive in me. The performer, wanting to sing, is very much alive. [Bill sings lead in the project.] But the drummer lies still, and he's very patient."

OZZY OSBOURNE

Ozzy used…well, whatever microphone might be handy. He did mention using an electronic doubler – an ADT box – for live performances to thicken the sound. The truth is that John could have sung through a paper cup on a string and he'd still be Ozzy. As Bill pointed out so many times, Osbourne was not a great singer but a wonderful conveyor of emotions and sensations. The technical side holds about as much interest for him as a headless dove. It's the live fowl that captures his attention.

"The most ironic thing is with all this fucking digital technology. You'd be surprised at how many guys go to me, 'How did you get that sound on *Volume 4*? How did you get the sound on the first Black Sabbath album?' The first album was recorded in twelve hours on two four-track machines in a little garage studio. It proves a point to me that everybody is driving technology forward, yet they still want to know how we got the old sound in the late '60s/early '70s. You stick *Sergeant Pepper* on there and it still sounds fucking great. The proof is in the pudding. You could put a record on from the '60s and you *know* it's from the '60s.

"On *Ozzmosis*, Michael Beinhorn would come in and run into me and go, 'Look at this. Isn't that fantastic?' And I'd go, 'It's a microphone.' And he'd say, 'But do you know *what* microphone?' And I'd go, 'I don't know, Michael.' And he'd tell me what it was and then I'd go, 'Michael, I don't mean to offend you but I still don't know.'"

12 Sin-cerely –
Ex-Ozzy Guitar Players Mouth Off

This brief section is intended to shed a bit more light on the working personality of Ozzy Osbourne. He has remained at the forefront of hard rock since he first bared his tonsils, over 25 years ago. He has taken sabbaticals, performed some outrageous and genuinely stupid and uncaring acts and performed in concert looking like an over-inflated caricature doll, and yet he consistently sells records and tickets and manages to hold onto an audience as fickle as Liz Taylor.

Perhaps his greatest talent is in choosing musicians, guitarists in particular. When he left Black Sabbath, the singer had no band, no music and an uncertain future, but he miraculously assembled a group around the late Randy Rhoads, recording just two albums, *Blizzard Of Ozz* and *Diary Of A Madman*, and from that point on became sort of a perverted Pied Piper, attracting known and unknown players to strum his ever-changing styles of music.

These, then, are the words of Ozzy's sidemen, those chosen to stand in the huge shoes vacated by Rhoads and, before him, Iommi. Unfortunately, I never had a chance to meet with Randy before his death on 19 March 1982.

BRAD GILLIS

"Playing with Ozzy was an…experience. He was a really great guy. He treated me well, but it took a while for him to accept me. [The ex-Night Ranger played on but one album, the November 1982 live recording *Speak Of The Devil*, from the Ritz Club in New York.] After he did, he treated me real well, and he was all for it. He gave me total freedom to do what I wanted. The first guitarist to join Ozzy [following Randy's death] was Bernie Tormé.* I guess he was pretty much told what to play and what to do, and he really didn't seem to work out. When I came in [Gillis was referred to Ozzy by guitarist Pat Thrall, who used to play with Tommy Aldridge, Osbourne's drummer], I just put in everything I could and tried to stay in the same vein for all the solos but also tried to branch out in my own style, so I pretty much had a handle on it and wasn't coaxed on how to do this or that. He gave me pretty much complete freedom, and I was real happy with that, because I could pretty much do anything I wanted.

But there was a big hassle with Randy Rhoads because, when they started doing Black Sabbath material, Randy didn't want to play any of the old Tony Iommi guitar licks, because they were so stock and basic. He thought he could put some style into it, and Ozzy didn't like that. He wanted him to stick to the basics. I guess finally, after a while, he was able to get through that and was able to do a little more. And when I started playing that stuff, [Ozzy] never said a word. I was able to do anything I wanted. When

***

* An Irish-born player who formed his own band, The Urge, in 1976. He later played with Scrapyard, The Bernie Tormé Group and Ian Gillan's band, Gillan. He played with Ozzy for two weeks, then went on to assemble Electric Gypsies and, in 1988, teamed up with ex-Twisted Sister vocalist Dee Snider under the name Desperado.

we did the live album, he said, 'Do anything you want to do. Go for it.' And everything just kind of fell into place.

"But Ozzy was cool. He came down when we were cutting our album [*Dawn Patrol*, February 1983] with Sharon and hung out with us. He's a real decent guy, real fun. In fact, there was an article in *Kerrang!* magazine that said Ozzy was on our album singing back-up, which he wasn't. We told him we'd pay him triple scale if he'd come in and sing. We wanted to get his voice on the album so kids would pick it up, so I guess the word got out that he did that, but he didn't.

"From the top, when I joined Ozzy, it was a temporary thing, just finishing off a couple weeks of touring, and I was worried whether Night Ranger would ever get signed [the quintet didn't yet have their deal on Boardwalk Records], so I was working my hardest to keep this gig with Ozzy, because it was definitely a great gig. And then we finally got a record deal and Sharon made me a really ridiculous deal to stay, and I was all confused about what to do. My heart was with Night Ranger, but here I am with the number one touring act. I was confused, but all of a sudden this album started taking off, so it was obvious what I had to do. It was hard to make the decision, but it had to be done, so I gave him my notice."

JAKE E LEE (NÉ JAKEY LOU WILLIAMS)
"On *Bark At The Moon* [the first Ozzy album on which Jake appeared, December 1983], I approached it really cautiously, because I was the new guy and I could be out any second, so I just played him riffs and if he liked the riff then the whole band would work on it. I didn't argue

too much, if I didn't like the way something was coming out. I'd go, 'I don't really like this.' And they'd go, 'Well, what do you know?' And I'd go [in a sheepish voice], 'I don't know anything.'

"The strings on 'Bark At The Moon' I hated. 'So Tired' I hated. I'd present something and they'd fight, debate, say it sucked or whatever. Everybody contributed a little bit, and it didn't necessarily come out the way I imagined it would. On *The Ultimate Sin* [February 1986], while Ozzy was in the Betty Ford Clinic, I got a drum machine, one of those mini-studios, a bass from Charvel – a really shitty one – and I more or less wrote entire songs. Sometimes I'll write something weird that I think he'll like and he'll say, 'That's too weird. Are you on acid or something? This isn't Frank Zappa.' And I'll write something simple that I think he might like and he'll go, 'That's pop. What is it?'

"Someone contacted me about the spot in Ozzy's band, and at first I said no, because I didn't want to step into Randy Rhoads' shoes. It's hard enough trying to replace a good guitar player, and I don't want this to sound callous but, when they die, they turn into a legend, and that's really tough. I didn't want that. But I went down there anyway. I think there was a list of 25 guitarists, and we all spent 15 minutes in the studio, each doing whatever we wanted to do. We had our pictures taken and they were given to Ozzy and he picked three of us. George Lynch [Dokken] was one of them, and he was given first crack at it and flown to England, and there was me and Mitch Perry left in LA. Ozzy came down and we auditioned at SIR [Studio Instrument Rentals] and I got it. I was 45 minutes late. Some guy said Ozzy almost walked out the door. He said, 'Fuck it. If this guy doesn't care enough to show up on time and he's going to be this kind of problem, forget it. I don't care how good he is.'

"People have sometimes wondered if I felt obscured, playing in Ozzy's band, but if anything I think I get more attention than I deserve as a guitarist. If somebody comes up to me and goes, 'Man you're number one, you're the best guitar player in the world,' I start feeling stupid. I go, 'Nah. There are guys better than me.' But if somebody comes up and says, 'You really suck, you're nothing compared to Randy,' then I go, 'Hey, fuck you. I'm good. I'm probably ten times better than you'll ever be.' No, I never felt obscured at all. As long as it sounded good, Ozzy didn't care."

Zakk Wylde (né Zach Adams)

"When I first joined Ozzy, I was still listening to heavy shit, and obviously songs by The Eagles and Skynyrd were too major sounding to work with Ozzy. Heavy metal stuff gets all minory, although the Allmans play a lot of stuff that was dark, darker than Skynyrd. If you do get those country bends happening in an Ozzy song, playing those Dickie Betts licks, you'd get one of those looks from Ozzy and he'd say, 'What the fuck does *that* mean? You're kidding, aren't you?' If I showed Ozzy a song like 'Losin' Your Mind' from my record [*Pride And Glory*], he'd smash the banjo over my head and say, 'Save it for your own record, Zakk.'

"On *No More Tears* [October 1991], we'd just go in and jam some stuff. I had some ideas from working at home and I thought it would be a cool idea for Ozzy, and he'd pick the songs he liked and sing something over it. But Ozzy never forced me to do anything. When I first started playing with Ozzy and doubled something, it's like when you first double your voice – the first time, you go, 'Man, it sounds killer!' The first time I doubled my guitars, it sounded awesome. It fits great with that style of music.

"With Ozzy, it's Ozzy music and has to fit into his thing. I mean, those songs were me, too, but 'No More Tears' doesn't totally sound like a country song. But then, a tune like, 'Mama, I'm Coming Home' could have ended up on my album. It even has that country thing in the beginning.

"Ozzy will always be part of my life. He's the godfather of my child, and he knew I was always going to do something on my own. I've learned a lot from him, about making records and everything, but at the end of the day, making records is just going in and playing. I learned how to drink lots of beer with Ozzy."

JOE HOLMES
"I took lessons from Randy [Rhoads] when I was about 16 or 17 years old. It's really weird, very strange. Those two *Blizzard Of Ozz* albums were a big part of me when I was growing up, and here I am playing a lot of it. The thing is, Ozzy is really a great person. He's even telling me, like in 'Suicide Solution', just to be myself and do my thing. He's really cool. He lets you dress the way you want to dress and just do your thing. He makes you feel comfortable with it because he's encouraging.

"I'll get my real chance with him when I get to play on a record with him. [Zakk Wylde handles guitar duties on the *Ozzmosis* album.] That's when you can be yourself, when you can write with him and do your thing. Until then, you're playing live and playing for people. On all the Sabbath songs, I keep them open and improvise during all the solo sections, just screw around and do whatever I want to do, but on the songs that people come to hear, like 'Mr Crowley' and 'Goodbye To Romance' and 'I Don't Know', you've got to play those the right way. Like on 'Flying High Again', how could I ever change that solo?

"I first heard about the Ozzy gig around '94, when they were writing or doing the record. Mike Inez [Ozzy's old bassist and now in Alice In Chains] called me and told me they were looking for someone. At the time, I was in LA in a band and we were right in the middle of doing demos for Warner Bros, so I was staying with what I had. And then [drummer] Dean Castronovo called me about three months ago and told me about the gig. My band were starting to showcase and do our thing, but I wanted to go do it. Out of anything, any gig, if I ever had to play with somebody, this would be it for me. And then, about two months ago, they called again and I went down and just played. I did 'I Don't Know' and 'Mr Crowley' and 'Bark At The Moon' and 'Crazy Train', and that was it for that day. Ozzy said, 'Welcome aboard.'

"Playing with Dean and Geezer is fun. They lock it in and set such a groove that...how can you go out? We go up there and attack it. You do a song like 'War Pigs' and you look over and see Geezer's fingers flying and go,

'Wow!', and see Ozzy standing there singing. There's a lot of breathing room, and with this rhythm section they lay it down so heavy, it's really nice. It's thick and fat sounding. It's huge.

"I think one thing about me playing with Ozzy is that I bring a little bit of the alternative to the music. I think that's one thing they like about me, because I'm really into all of that, like the Alice In Chains sound. I think I can really bring a different side into it. I've always wanted to do something I'm really proud of, and I know, if I ever had to pick a singer [for a solo project] while I was growing up, it was always Ozzy. A lot of these newer bands have all been influenced by that Sabbath stuff, so I really think I'd be myself and be proud of a record I did with Ozzy. Why would you want to do a solo record if you were doing what was representing you already?

"I just go up there and play. When I did the thing with Dave [Lee Roth – Holmes replaced Jason Becker in October 1990 for live dates] and went to Europe, I knew Steve [Vai] and Eddie [Van Halen] were rated number one and were really respected, and that was good for me, to get out there in front of those crowds and play. You've just gotta go up there and have a good time with it. Hopefully, I'll get a good response. You've just gotta do your thing. Not everyone will like you. I'm gonna go up there and kick the shit out of the guitar, eat 'em up. I'll do a good job with it. Ozzy checked a lot of guys out before he chose me, and I want those guys to come and watch. Heck, yeah. I'd rather go and watch a good guy than someone who's not. When I go and see a band or a guitar player, I want to see someone who's inspiring, who's gonna make me go home and play the guitar. I don't feel a competition thing with anyone. I'm just gonna go and do my thing."

STEVE VAI (BRIEFLY REHEARSED/COMPOSED WITH OZZY)
"To a greater or lesser degree, I am a heavy metal knucklehead. I've been known to knucklehead around with heavy metal. But I have this whole other side, Dr Jekyll and Mr Steve. So, to half of Steve Vai, it was odd that Ozzy would call, but then, to the other half, it was, 'Well, why should it be odd? I play heavy metal. I enjoy it.' Ozzy is moving on to icon-ness, and I'm right up his alley, in the sense that I'm not a young 19-year-old Mongolian string-bender. I've been around. So it was a good idea, and we got some great, great stuff. But, unfortunately, there's a hierarchy involved here, and it's the record company that makes the decisions.

"If things had worked out and a tour came up, in the beginning I would not have stayed. But, after I met Ozzy, I really started to like him a lot. He was a lot of fun all the time. And then I started thinking, 'Yeah, I would definitely go out on a world tour thing with this guy.' Before that, I'd had it up to here with rock 'n' roll singers [having worked with David Lee Roth and David Coverdale in Whitesnake], but he was really different. I don't mean that in a nasty way against the guys I worked with; I just wanted to do my own thing.

"The way this whole thing happened was that Ozzy had recorded with his band and the band sort of went off and did different things, so they needed a few more songs to record, and so they got together with me. It was very weird that there was gonna be two guitarists on the record [*Ozzmosis*]. Half of it was gonna be Zakk and half of it was gonna be me. So I wrote a bunch of stuff with Ozzy, some great stuff, and we had a lot of laughs. He's really a pretty wild guy. But it turned out the record company liked some of the material and they didn't like some of it, so they set Ozzy up with a lot of other writers [Bryan Adams' main collaborator Jim Vallance and Aerosmith insider Mark Hudson]. Due to time and finances, they thought the best idea was to get Zakk to finish the record. But now Ozzy and I have a whole stockload of material and we hope to use some of it someday. It's just that right now isn't the right time."

Ideally, what these Osbourne sidekicks have revealed allows for a better understanding of the singer himself. We'll let him close the doors on this verbal vault with a few words of his own.

"When Randy died, I was looking for somebody with a lot of spark, somebody with a bit of go in them, 'cause the thing is, if you go and audition a guy and you rehearse with the guy, there's no rehearsal better than a gig. That's always been my philosophy. As soon as Randy was killed, I had the awful task of finding someone. And the first guy was great at rehearsal, but when he got on stage he just shit. It was, like, 'Fuck, what's this ocean of people?' I mean, it's a big step for somebody who's been playing in bars to go in front of 18,000 kids. He would just freeze and couldn't handle it. That's the hardest part, to find a guy who can handle the situation. Randy was a gem, because he was a great player, a great person and a great performer, and he loved being on stage. It was a unique combination. He was a natural. I know in the first five minutes of playing with a guy whether he's cool, over-cool or too smart. It's just a gift or something. Randy was the most refreshing player.

"There's a million good players out there. You've just got to find them, and that takes a bit of time. It's like there are so many name people that think, 'Well, I can't use Joe Blow, 'cause he's nothing. I've got to get Eric Clapton or I've got to get Jimmy Page.' Jimmy Page was discovered by somebody else, but I'll never use a name guitar player to work with, if I can help it. First of all, you've got to deal with their ego, because they're the biggest thing in the world. I can't stand to work with people with egos. If anyone works in the band and starts to cop an ego, I have to get rid of them, because an ego will spread through a band faster than the plague. You've just got to keep it level, and the reason that I kept going all the time was that I think I don't sound that great. I mean, there's always someone out there greater than me. I just had a great, lucky break. I'm a lucky man. I realise it all.

"There's so many people that think, 'Sniff this, shove this up your ass, drink that,' and you're cool, but they're fucking insane. It's like shoving your head in the sand and waiting for the storm to pass. I went through all that. I've grown out of all that crap. I lived with it for eleven years. When Sabbath were so drug-orientated for a while, it was like, 'How you doing [sniff]?' We used to sniff, 'Morning!' to each other. It was so crazy. It's like you experiment with it all, and you either grow out of it or you don't, or it grows out of you and you end up in a fucking box. The pace of living in this kind of a life is like 300 miles per hour. It's like racing. You get to a point where you suffer from a thing I invented called adrenalinosis. You've got so much adrenalin that you can't do anything. You've got to take a drink to cool it down. It's okay going freaky if you've got something to offer with what you're doing. I mean, I've stood my ground. I believed in what I did.

"I did crazy things. I was kind of drunk one day and I was pissed off with these white-shirted people looking at me as a fucking can of beans to sell, and so I bit the head off a bird. I'll do anything on the spur of the moment. That's why I should have been on that plane when it went down with Randy in it, without a shadow of doubt. I just thought, 'Fuck, it's fate.' I believe that fate takes his hand, you know? Then there was the funeral and half a dozen groupies were in the church. It was like a fucking Fellini movie, a bad dream. Fucking life at the top, you know?

"The music has always meant a lot to me, but I felt somewhat like a mouse on a wheel, going around in circles. As the years were going by, I was getting very bogged in, as far as my success went, in the respect of the image I had created – Ozzy Osbourne with blood dripping out of his mouth. You would never expect anything else of me. I wanted to vent a lot of other ideas. If it wasn't *Bark At The Moon* or *Diary Of A Madman*, with me being the monster that I created, no one would want it. So the title of my new album was an idea I had about forming a completely new band and calling the album *Ozzmosis*. [Webster's defines 'osmosis' in its most rigid translation as 'the diffusion of fluids through a membrane'.] It's like two liquid molecules going through a solid object, coming out and finding another one, a kind of rebirth. In the three years that I had been off the road [since *No More Tears*, September 1991], that period gave me a chance to be a father and to actually live in a house for a while, to be in one place and appreciate where I am, what I'm about. It's like the old saying goes: 'You never know what you've had until you've lost it.' I worked with Steve Vai and we wrote together. I'd love to do an album with Steve. He's a wonderful guy. I had a great time with him. And then I found Joe Holmes.

"I'm glad I'm still here. I'm still very insecure with myself, and I think that's what keeps me motivated. I either pull it off or I don't. Looking back, the '70s, in my opinion, was the best music. The '70s, without any shadow of a doubt, were great, because there was no MTV and, if you wanted to see a band, you bought a record and the whole surprise was to see what the band were like. A lot of people didn't know where we were from, who we were. We didn't do many press interviews, we never did any radio and we certainly didn't do any TV. We never sat down in 1970 and said, 'Man, when we write this album, in the year 1995 people are going to look at this as a masterpiece.' We were four fucked-up kids who had this big machine to play with. If I hadn't done that first Black Sabbath album, I wouldn't be sitting here now talking to you. That was the diving board for Ozzy Osbourne to leap off into this wonderful world. Thank God for that first Black Sabbath album.

I just don't want to be remembered for biting heads off living creatures. I've done a lot more positive things since then.

"But if the chance came up to record with the original band again, would I? No."

13 From Then To Eternity

At the end of the previous chapter, when questioned whether he would ever perform with the original members of the band again, Ozzy Osbourne responded with a resounding no. He'd had enough. He'd played too many concerts, raised the Richard Nixon-inspired double-handed peace sign far too many times, had recorded too many songs and was just generally worn out, both physically and inspirationally, by a routine that had gone on for so many gruelling years. However, in 1996, shortly after he made this statement, his outlook would change. A reunion with the seminal characters was on the horizon and new music was in the process of being written and digested. Verbal promises uttered by rock icons and politicians are about as reliable as a used condom, and not to be trusted, but during the five-plus years when the one-time slaughterhouse attendant and convicted thief made this statement, a world of changes would ensue.

Let's back up just a touch to put things in full focus. The band had recorded *Forbidden*, an album featuring rapper-turned-rocker Ice T. This was the first time that a guest vocalist had ever been brought in to assist with tracks. Ozzy, of course, had been out of the picture for some time, but a linking-up with his original band mates was not far off. Ice T sang on the track 'Illusion Of Power', and it's more than likely that he mentioned his guitarist, Ernie C, as a possible candidate to produce the record. The band – made up of vocalist Tony Martin, guitarist Tony Iommi, bassist Neil Murray, drummer Cozy Powell and keyboardist Geoff Nicholls – hit the streets in support of the album, but an utter lack of support by the IRS mother label resulted in less-than-sparkling ticket sales.

Drummer Cozy Powell, in short order, would be replaced by Bobby Rondinelli. Rondinelli then completed the Forbidden tour, including Far East dates in Japan and Australia. These performances ended in December 1995, after which the band found itself walking in circles. Just a few months later, in April 1996, IRS Records, in an attempt to keep the Sabbath saga alive, released a compilation CD called *The Sabbath Stones*, a quasi-greatest hits (emphasis on *hits*) package of IRS-released tracks. Scrambling to fill up digital space, the label also included music from *Born Again*, *Seventh Star* and *Eternal Idol*. This represents the band's final gasp with IRS, and sources are quick to point out that Tony only allowed the making of this amalgam to fulfil final obligations. Looking from the other side, one might surmise that the band had lost its label and was desperately searching for a new one.

Rumours flew like bombers when word surfaced that ex-Judas Priest singer Rob Halford would accept the role as front lungsman. Apparently, Tony was seeking out singers to work with him on his solo album and Halford's name materialised. There were some perfunctory collaborations, but all of the material was shelved and Tony ended up spending the remainder of 1996 working on the album by himself. Glenn Hughes was another vocalist working with him at around this time and playing bass. This material resulted in the bootleggish *Eighth Star*. Diehards are still waiting for the Halford material.

Later in 1996, in October, another announcement was made about, yes, another band member departing, but this one was just a rumour. Players were working outside the Sabbath fold, and this is probably where the flags were first raised. Neil Murray was working with Cozy Powell in Peter Green's outfit and Bobby Rondinelli had been mixing it up with the Sun Red Sun group he had created with Ray Gillen. Gillen would later become another rock casualty, forcing the drummer to join forces with Blue Öyster Cult.

During this period, hearsay began to fly about concerning a reunion of the original band. In March 1997, word was spread about the foursome appearing at Ozzy's 1997 Ozzfest tour, a programme that the singer had assembled showcasing new and established purveyors of the metal style that he and his three Aston chums had conjured up several decades earlier. However, politics, passion and people skewed the original concept, and the metal gathering ended up with only Iommi, Osbourne and Butler appearing, with drummer Mike Bordin behind the drum kit. Apparently, Ozzy's wife/manager Sharon had cut Bill Ward off at the legs – or, more appropriately, at the hands – and told him that the invitation wasn't meant for him. She'd even sent a wire to the disappointed drummer addressing the issue and telling him why he would not be present. This missive was sent on 7 April 1997 to the Ozzy Osbourne discussion folder in American On-Line's music section:

Subj: Bill Ward
Date: Mon 7 Apr 1997 20:07:41 EST
From: World Of Ozz

This is Sharon Osbourne. I understand there has been quite a bit of uproar regarding Bill Ward not playing the Ozzfest with Black Sabbath. Bill was not asked to play on this bill due to inter-personal business conflicts between himself, me and Ozzy. It is a private issue that we have kept private out of respect to Bill. Bill doesn't understand that we are only trying to protect him. We will announce the reason why he wasn't asked to do this tour.

We appreciate all of your support in this matter and ask that everyone just be grateful that you will have the opportunity to see Sabbath and just try to enjoy the concert. We are doing this for YOU – OUR FANS.

Thank you

Sharon and Ozzy

Bill, understandably, was crushed. This almost-original line-up played about a one-hour set at Ozzfest as a finale, following Ozzy's solo appearance. The foursome would remain intact for a mere two months, until the beginning of July, but that period represented a weight that Bill Ward would carry for a very long time.

He first heard about the Ozzfest upon seeing Tony and Geezer on MTV. Having just returned from rehearsals with his own band, he saw his supposed comrades on television making the announcement and his initial reaction was, justifiably, one of "deep sadness". The MTV announcement came on a Friday, and for the duration of the weekend the soft-spoken and even-tempered drummer tried to work through his emotions and make some sense of what was happening. Three faxes were delivered – one to Tony, one to Gloria Butler and the last to Ernest Chapman (Iommi's representative and long-time manager of Jeff Beck), in which he cleaved open his own chest to reveal a broken heart.

The pain emanated from the hurt dispensed by Tony's and Geezer's go-along attitude. He couldn't believe that these two people – especially the former – nailed him to the cross in such an unthinking fashion without even bestowing upon him the courtesy of a phone call or explanation of any sort. Ernest Chapman, in fact, was the most understanding. He sent a return fax confirming that the guitarist and bassist were involved in this modified reunion and the show was a done deal. Confronted with this very real admission, Bill was able to catalogue his feelings in a more non-emotional way.

Sharon did phone him, reiterating what was revealed in the original print message – hammering home the fact that his services were not required – but all Bill really wanted to know was how Tony and Geezer felt. There was no begging for the job. As much as he would have loved to have been there, he understood that this was Ozzy's show and that no provision had been made for his inclusion. By Monday, he had tempered his anger and upset, and on St Patrick's Day he said a prayer for them and intoned to himself that Black Sabbath would be nevermore.

This entire event came as no real surprise, since Sharon had let it be known for over a year that she would never permit Ward to rejoin the original band. On that day in 1997, in Bill's mind, the original Sabbath would never again play music together.

Following the Ozzfest dates, everyone went about taking care of their own business: Ozzy jumped on his greatest hits package, *The Ozzman Cometh*, and set about bringing that to a close; Geezer stayed on the road in support of his *Black Science* solo endeavour; and Tony continued working on his solo album. But rumours continued to persist unabated about a true regrouping. Those purportedly in the know said that English dates had even been inked in for December 1987. Sharon Osbourne, tongue in cheek, called Bill about flying to Europe to rehearse for gigs, ostensibly booked on 4 and 5 December, but Bill, having been bitten more times than a beekeeper without a bonnet, was wary. He explained that, while he had not been "contracted" to play, he had been invited to "rehearse". The music business, as has been mentioned throughout this book, is based on perception, innuendo and intent. Facts and the truth are stomped like cigarette butts. Tickets had already been printed hailing the "Original Black Sabbath" and were put on sale, and yet Ward hadn't signed any papers indicating his participation.

Nonetheless, Bill flew to England on or around 11 November to begin work. As a sort of hedge – and maybe some plant conjured up by management – MTV announced an injury to Ward's hand, indicating that he might not be able to appear for these dates. This was a lie. However, on 24 November, the periodicals stated that the original quartet would play dates on 4 and 5 December. The shows were recorded – both audio and video – for ostensible release dates later in 1998. The video would ultimately see light as the *Reunion* video.

Even with all this hoopla over the coming-together of the four Sabbath boys, the dates represented a sort of flawed originality. Keyboardist Geoff Nicholls provided backing music, and as we all know, Geoff wasn't on those first albums. But the gigs were played and everyone went their separate ways. Then, in March 1988, there was an announcement of a double live album to be completed and marketed around Halloween of that year.

No one involved in the reunion was blind or immune in any way to the potential of what might lie ahead. Although the band had gone through dozens of personnel, none came close to the Osbourne/ Iommi/Butler/Ward roster. So, with a couple of dates behind them – the first time the four had performed together in virtually two and a half decades – additional concerts were arranged for June 1988. Work began *circa* 14 May.

The world of music is a precarious one based on a foundation of lies, larceny and ravenous lawyers, and musicians themselves – creatures of habits, often bad – are susceptible to the lures and immediate gratifications of quick money and quick women. They are fragile beings, tend to be over-indulgent and rarely think about consequences. With all of this working for them – or, more appropriately, against them – it's a stone-cold wonder that music is ever composed or completed. It should therefore come as no real surprise that, while rehearsing, Bill Ward suffered a mild heart attack. As is common knowledge, the drummer was a heavy drinker and abuser of drugs and was a bit overweight, and so an aortic attack shouldn't have come as a surprise to anyone. Doctors forced him to recuperate for a period of six weeks, during which time Vinnie Appice flew in from America as a fill-in.

Ward recovered and began working with his own Bill Ward Band. In the meantime, the *Reunion* album was released, on 20 October, and to commemorate this long-time-coming musical reunion the four musicians embarked on an eight-city in-store signing tour, on which they signed copies of the album and various other mementos brought along by their fans. These various record-store locations turned into serious mob scenes where fans, deprived of seeing the real members together for so many years, jostled and pushed and virtually stampeded security in order to secure personal autographs. These stores, typically of the mega-chain variety – Tower, Virgin *et al* – had established a policy that, in order to have an album signed, you were required to purchase a copy of *Reunion* at that moment. Many of the faithful had already bought a copy, but these corporate monsters, absolutely insensitive to the feelings of the awaiting throng, paid them no heed. You were guaranteed to have one of the four apply ink to your album if you bought a copy. Even so, many of these people who shelled out the money were turned away. They were justifiably livid and tossed invectives at the band and the record management.

There were even rumours that the band was going to play secret club gigs, but these turned out to be unadulterated lies. However, they did assemble for one live set, an appearance on *The David Letterman Show*, on which they covered 'Paranoid'.

Fuelled, perhaps, by this one-off showing, they then assembled for a series of radio station spots – in essence, promos for the *Reunion* album. With these media spots in the can, the band once again retired to their various homes. However, in December 1998, they began rehearsals for what would be the 1999 Reunion tour, a journey that would kick off on New Year's Eve in Phoenix, Arizona. By now, no Sabbath trek was without its problems, and, true to form, two dates were postponed. Shows in Salt Lake City, Utah, and Denver, Colorado, were put on hold due to illness. ('Flu was the reason given.) Sensing impending disaster, the band once again tapped Vinnie Appice as surrogate stand-in, should Bill Ward go down. Appice's set was assembled at the back of the stage, behind Bill's, and the drummer was ready to step in at a moment's notice.

But Ward was back and strong and determined, and Appice did little more than warm the bench. Bill played with emotion and drive and the tour was generally regarded as one of substance and soul. Although the band hadn't mixed it up for over two decades, the magic was still there. The only criticism levelled at them was regarding their set list, which didn't vary from night to night. *Master Of Reality* was the record from which they drew most of the material. 'Psycho Man', a new piece they had worked out, was not included in the show, and this disappointed everyone. Still, reviews and response to this tour was unanimously positive.

With Ward now healthy, someone had to take the fall, and this time it was Ozzy. During the middle of the tour, the singer developed a throat nodule, a tiny yet irritating growth on the larynx, and once again several shows were postponed. Osbourne took time off to rest up and resumed touring, but continuing throat problems resulted in many cancelled dates and even the multiple postponement of select concerts.

However, buoyed by the response, the band decided to headline 1999's Ozzfest. In April 1999, Sharon billed this tour as "the Last Supper", the group's final performance. Ozzy suffered more vocal emergencies, but the Ozzfest date came off without a hitch. The final shows were held at the NEC in Birmingham in December, when Ozzy maintained steadfastly that these would be the last shows that the four originals would ever perform. (Some seven years earlier, the singer had promised his own retirement, and we now know that that was but a falsehood. So, too, these final dates proved to be anything but.)

In 2000, the band was relatively quiet, although the guitarist finally released his own self-titled solo album. Released on 17 October 2001, the album contains ten tracks and finds the left-handed guitarist teamed up with a variety of auxiliary singers and players. Co-produced by Ralph Baker and Bob Marlette, *Iommi* first took shape back in 1996, when the picker wrote with Glenn Hughes, Dave Holland and Don Airey. All of that work was set aside, however, and Tony began anew. (Some of these tracks are available on a bootleg called *Eighth Star*.) This album actually represents his second official solo outing, if you count 1986's *Seventh Star*, recorded during a Sabbath hiatus.

Tony made it clear from the beginning that he wanted to use outside voices to shape the sound and called upon singers such as Phil Anselmo, Billy Corgan, Ozzy, Billy Idol, Serj Tankian (System Of A Down), Peter Steele (Type O Negative), Ian Astbury, Dave Grohl, Skin (Skunk Anansie) and Henry Rollins. In addition to these various crooners, he brought in former Soundgarden bassist Ben Shepherd and veteran drummers Matt Cameron, Kenny Aranoff, Dave Grohl, John Tempesta, Bill Ward and Jimmy Copely. Even Queen maestro Brian May adds his magic on 'Goodbye Lament', the Grohl track, and burns through a solo on 'Flame On', the Ian Astbury song. He told *Guitar World*, "We've put the Sabbath thing on hold for the time being, but if something comes along that seems right for us, we'll do it. I'd love to do something again. We all really enjoy playing together."

In fact, everyone was working on their own particular projects. Bill had been putting the finishing touches on *Beyond Aston*, a nod to the days of innocence. As he did on *When The Bough Breaks*, the drummer coloured the music with elements ranging from accordion and choir to a complete orchestra for one track. The title track was penned as an ode to Ozzy, a piece he wrote over ten years ago. "I'm trying different things," explained Ward in a recent interview. "'I think I've improved a little bit between my feet and my arms and my head. I'm trying to put extra little things in. By the time we'd finished with the Sabbath tours and the Ozzfest tours in 1999, I felt pretty good about my drumming. It felt that it was starting to awaken, and I thought, "Well, you're having a good time here.' I was starting to put some jazz chops in between all the hard rock. So I was enjoying doing that. I don't think the audience could ever hear it, but I was having a blast doing it. It just kept everything nice."

Geezer has meanwhile been sculpting out the form for his third solo album. One song included is called 'The Ultimate Ghost', a nod, perhaps, to the seemingly endless career of his main band. He believes it is his most definitive work to date. As he laid out in a conversation, "I've got about twelve songs done. It encompasses everything I've done. Right now, Clark Brown has done all the vocals, and I'm working with Pedro Howse again, who was the guitarist on my last two albums."

Several tracks may make their way onto the new Sabbath album. He maintains that the record is a return to roots, the '70s sound. Quick to point out that the new material sounds nothing like the *Reunion* music, he describes the working process as resembling what they did on the first three Sabbath albums – simply sitting in the studio, jamming, recording everything that came out and then allowing the songs to sit for a period and revisiting them to choose what hopefully represented a new sound. Ozzy would then work up vocal melodies. Also, the bassist is not the designated in-house lyricist –

all of the other three members proffered ideas and, if they reached a unanimous decision, work continued.

The material, at this date, is still in an embryonic stage. There are no completed lyrics. That's always the last undertaking. However, there are three or four songs that, according to the bassist, are "ready to record". One song evolved as a radio-friendly ballad and was dumped immediately, reeking of commercialism. Fortunately, there is no rush to complete the record, since it represents an extraordinary milestone for the band – their first studio collaboration in over 20 years.

Bill is also excited about the new music, citing it as "pretty melodic, definitely hard rock". He realises that it's a good start for a band that hasn't officially written together for such a long time: "I feel that the beginning shows incredible potential and promise. There are some slower songs which actually have some jazz and real melodic feel, and there's a real melodic one that I was going to say is almost like 'Changes', but in a rhythm sense it's nothing like 'Changes'. It really complements Ozzy's lament voice. There's something that is just totally awesome about his voice, when he sings sad songs. It just turns out so great. Then we have something that is just so tight and up-tempo and total fucking metal. So the range is quite wide. We've just started to tap the motherlode. There's potentially enough material to go for a long, long time, not just for one album. It's very exciting. There are a lot of different ideas."

In late June, the group appeared at a Weenie Roast for Los Angeles radio station KROQ. Ozzy was scheduled to perform as a solo act but brought along Bill, Geezer and Tony. The itinerary had them playing three songs, but after Iommi's amplifier blew up they were forced to forego the third selection.

And now, in 2001, the band are still in the game. They headlined this year's version of the Ozzfest and actually have plans to release a new studio album. As of this writing, no title has been chosen, although there is a projected release date sometime in 2002, and on this recording the four players will be augmented by keyboardist Geoff Nicholls. The principals began work during March and April of 2001, assembling ideas in an English studio. The original plan was to complete the Ozzfest 2001 dates and then return to the studio in early September to put finishing touches on it in order to have it ready for the Christmas 2001 holiday season. However, insistent pressure from Ozzy's label to complete his own album resulted in the shelving of the project until January 2002.

Zakk Wylde, Ozzy's long-standing guitar brother, is also involved with the project. He reveals that Ozzy has gone to outside writers for material, and Wylde, leader of his own Black Label Society (their new album is called *Alcohol-Fuelled Brewtality Live*, on Spitfire Records), is not completely in agreement with that decision. He told *Guitar World*, "Most of what I've played on so far is stuff they had already worked on, including songs by a bunch of different writers, even that dude who writes for The Offspring. That cunt wouldn't know a heavy riff it if hit him in the head. I want it to be as slamming heavy as possible, and some of it definitely will be. I'm bringing in a bunch of pissing-razors songs, and we'll see what

Ozzy likes. Anything he passes on goes straight onto the next Black Label Society album."

Meanwhile, Rick Rubin has been tagged as producer, and the only available information is one track title, 'Scary Dreams'. In the meantime, the Ozzfest 2001 dates have been captured on a 65-minute, 16-track CD called *The Second Millennium: Now Hell Has A Soundtrack*. Sabbath is represented with 'The Wizard', while the remainder of the album sports tracks from the other Ozzfest participants.

What's truly remarkable about Black Sabbath is that, as seen in this chapter, the band is still such an essential piece of the metal landscape. Save for some brief touring, a live album and various solo projects, the group still commands and garners more journalistic ink and recognition than virtually all of their contemporaries – and there is a busload of contemporaries. Metal has splintered into several camps. There is rapcore/nu-metal, which combines riffing and rapping, baseball caps spun backwards, led by the likes of Limp Bizkit. Stoner metal sounds like a dead body being dragged along the pavement – it's slow, dirgelike and features guitars tuned down so that the strings wobble endlessly, bottom-heavy. Electric Wizard, Sea Of Green and Spirit Caravan are this style's main candidates. The sludge/doom purveyors present bleak, barren sounds without solos. (Witness Cathedral, Isis and Neurosis.) Thrash, meanwhile, is accelerated rock with a lot of stop and go, as strummed by Soilwork, Shadows Fall and The Haunted. Grindcore was established years ago with Napalm Death, featuring meth-driven riffs *à la* Cephalic Carnage, Nasum and

Benumb. Hardcore metal is speedy and not for the weak of heart, with Coalesce, Drowningman and Glassjaw leading the pack. Then there is death metal, which is typified by mid-tempo cleaver guitar riffs and classic drum riffs in the style of Zeppelin. Attire is T-shirt and jeans. (Witness Morbid Angel, Dying Fetus and Six Feet Under.) Black metal, meanwhile, combines the melodic sympathy of orchestrated pieces with arrogant, in-your-face sounds. Its purveyors – Mayhem, Emperor, Cradle Of Filth and others – sport fangs, chain-mail shirts and *de rigueur* pants. Math Metal utilises the brainy elements of rock – Satriani, for example – performed at twice the speed of most other branches, and this is the style of choice for Meshuggah, Cryptopsy and Goreguts. Prog/power metal surrounds itself with dragons, knights and a baroque style, and Hammerfall, Blind Guardian and Rhapsody are the bands who protect these damsels in distress. Another vein, ethno metal, uses indigenous instruments, as used by Puerto Rico's Puya, Brazil's Soulfly and Finland's Amorphis. And finally there is miscellaneous avant-hybrid metal, a branch that changes with each record. Its proponents try either to confuse the listener or to actually maintain a creative element. Mr Bungle, Candria and The Melvins are bands of this sort, constantly changing like chameleons.

All of this is meant to convey the everlasting staying power of Black Sabbath. Dozens of bands have regrouped only to find an audience lacking in interest, but Sabbath have maintained a history few other bands have been able to sustain. This may come down to the fact that, at the end of the day, the band enjoys what it does.

Obviously, they fight, disagree, get in each other's faces and have suffered serious medical problems, but ultimately they always regroup, find a way around the obstacles and manage to create another album, seek out a solution and hit the road once again. Thirty years ago, Geezer Butler wrote these lyrics for a track called 'Paranoid': "I tell you to enjoy life. I wish I could, but it's too late." Sabbath seem to have grasped this elementary principle and, after three decades of playing music together, they're still around. They deserve kudos. They did things their way and managed to do it creatively and earn a buck along the way. Good for them.

14 The Nature Of The Beast

In the past year or so, Ozzy Osbourne has been elevated from simple rock superstar to *cause célèbre*, an international icon on several levels, including television, politics and Hollywood. In main, the reason for this new-found popularity rests on the reality television show recently aired on the MTV music station. Called simply *The Osbournes*, the series takes a behind-the-screens look at the Osbourne family, lifting the veil, as it were, on the Wizard of Oz himself and his sometimes rambunctious but always outspoken family. Ozzy, now 53 years old, has been at the helm of both Black Sabbath and his own solo career for over 35 years and somehow (mainly through the prodding of wife/manager Sharon, one would think) has broadened his horizons to become an authentic media figure.

The Osbournes is part *The Addams Family*, part *Father Knows Best* and in large part unadulterated, unfiltered profanity. The family's menagerie of cats and dogs is regularly urinating and crapping on Ozzy's favourite vintage rugs and even in his own bed. When it comes to cussing wars, it's difficult to decide who has the filthiest mouth; Sharon, the undisputed queen of the cadre, the main shot caller, lets fly with the *fuck* invective with regularity, while her ooky, spooky, pampered children hold their own on all fronts. While the Oz is no stranger to the language of the foul, his part in all of this seems to be more as colour than main character. He responds to the moment rather than creating it.

The opening season began on 5 March 2002 and was initially booked for ten episodes, but the debut episode rated so highly that it became the most successful series opener in MTV's history. Normally, by the time a second show is aired on television, interest drops by a quarter; to the absolute delight of the bean counters at the music video station, the sophomore episode jumped from a 2.8 household rating to a 3.2. No one had an answer for the success. Airing at 10.30pm, a no-man's-hour for TV broadcasting, the show itself has nothing more to recommend it than garbage language, the futile attempts of Papa O trying to tell his children about the dangers of drink and drugs, wife Sharon insisting that she doesn't need the trappings of all the money he earns (while she goes off on shopping sprees at the toniest boutiques in town) and his plump yet seductively intriguing children yelling at each other and bringing over famous actor and musician friends at ungodly hours of the wee morning. But damn, it is one freaking funny show.

MTV found the key to the kooky kingdom while airing an episode of *Cribs*, a show that takes a look at the palaces in which rock stars reside. They realised Ozzy and his heavy-handed wife were the parents of two prime MTV viewers – Kelly, 17, and Jack,16. (There is an older daughter, Aimee, 19, who opted out of the limelight and retreated to a summer house to record music during the six-month shooting schedule.) While most kids didn't have a bat-biting millionaire dad, the show believed that rockers from Boise, Idaho, and Louisville, Kentucky, would watch a show about just such a family. They were right.

The Osbournes has turned the singer and his family name into a virtual goldmine for merchandisers and broadcasters. When questioned about the success of the show by another media outlet, he responded, "I don't fucking understand it." But he told me, "I just get fucking better with age." Indeed. His personal fortune hovers somewhere around $57 million, and if anyone wants to understand why he'd even agree to a second season, just look at the payday – the first ten episodes brought him a cheque for somewhere around $750,000 while the new season will bring in an unbelievable $20 million. Pundits say that this works out as about $17,000 per curse. The deal was negotiated by wife Sharon, a hardcore, no-nonsense business entrepreneur who takes no prisoners (she's been sued by several of Ozzy's musical sidemen) and who threatened to take the show to competing networks. MTV reluctantly agreed to her demands.

Make no mistake about it, Ms Osbourne is the queen bee on and off the set. Daughter of legendary rock star maker and breaker Don Arden, from whom she learned the ropes of the trade, she has not spoken with her father for many years. Arden, married to dancer Hope Arden, was one of the early agents-turned-promoters and was responsible for bringing American musicians – Little Richard, Jerry Lee Lewis, Gene Vincent, The Everly Brothers, Sam Cooke – over to England in the formative years of the industry. Later, as a manager, he worked with The Small Faces, The Electric Light Orchestra and even Jayne Mansfield. But, pedigree or not, the Ardens aren't exactly what you'd call close. When Sharon began managing Ozzy, she approached dear old Dad about signing the ex-Sabbath frontman to a record deal and he turned her down. Silence has been the language of their love for the past couple of decades.

She is protective of Ozzy in a motherly sort of fashion – she can chew him up and spit him over the coals if he even makes a mention about a live set design or costume change – but if anyone else takes a stab at him, the teeth and talons emerge and the red-headed lady turns into one serious presence. Apparently, there's a running feud between her and Ted Nugent. Nuge, the great loin-clothed one, said after watching an episode of the series that it made Ozzy look like a "blithering, hapless idiot". Sharon's response: "Why don't you go back in the fucking sausage factory?" before threatening to castrate the man. Nothing like the love of a good woman.

But she has good reason to protect her better half, as he now represents a multi-million-dollar industry. Ozzy has sold 38 million albums in the US alone, while his Dark Skies PlayStation game is earning *la familia* bagfuls of green. He is the third most requested artist on rollingstone.com, behind Britney Spears and TLC (according to the 20 June 2002 issue of the magazine). And Ozzfest, the now *de rigueur* tour for upcoming and established bands of the ultra-heavy metal style, is in its seventh year and now represents an international travelcade, with the lion's share of the profits filtering directly into the Osbournes' coffers.

Just one week after the show's debut, Ozzy's latest album, *Down To Earth* [Epic], vaulted 52 spots on *SoundScan*'s Top Current Album chart to Number 93. And *The Ozzman Cometh: Greatest Hits* [Epic] was jacked up to Number Four on *Billboard*'s Top Pop Catalogue Albums chart, with this year's version also including System Of A Down, Adema, POD, Zakk Wylde's Black Label Society (Zakk also doubles as Ozzy's six-string sideman, but exhaustion forced him off some of the 2002 dates), Andrew WK, Rob Zombie, Drowning Pool, Meshuggah, lostprophets, Apex Theory, Pulse Ultra, OTEP, Chevelle, Seether, Neurotica, Ill Niño and others.

The success of the show has brought him to the attention of pre-series non-initiates, those who knew no more about Ozzy Osbourne than that he drank blood, engaged in daily sacrifices and was a falling-down drunk barely capable of stringing together two coherent sentences in cadence. Well, he has stopped the vampirism and it's doubtful that he ever killed anything (except maybe his own liver and brain cells), he no longer drinks (although he will mix one from time to time), and the grammar? A bit unintelligible, but always honest and usually so bone-dry funny you want to wet yourself with the delivery.

So he has now entered the arena of politics and was recently invited to the George W Bush White House Correspondents' Association Dinner, where he posed for pictures with the President, chummed it up with local scribes and politico journalists and generally seemed to have a grand old time.

He has also done the talk-show circuit, appeared in virtually every major newspaper in America and is now about to invade the rest of the world with his reality TV show. And, like all things huge, the trickle-down function means that these drops from heaven have hit the Osbourne children as well – Jack was hired by Epic as a talent scout (not a huge leap when you consider the sway Ozzy must now hold over his mother label) and has apparently been responsible for finding bands like Meshuggah, Soil and Adema as underdog Ozzfest additions.

While Jack followed his mother into the business aspect of making music, sister Kelly turned to Daddy and has started performing. She recorded a demo, ostensibly with sister Aimee (who apparently bowed out), with Jack as producer, travelling to New York to cut Madonna's 'Papa Don't Preach' with Incubus as backing band. The track was intended to be included on the soundtrack to *The Osbournes* (released on 21 May 2002) but, after disputes with band management and record-label people, the Incubus version was shelved and Kelly re-cut the song with other musicians. Surprisingly – or perhaps not so surprisingly, considering the gene pool – she created a frenzied and more than competent vocal presentation of the topical song.

The album featuring Kelly's debut is called *The Osbourne Family Album* and contains a rather intriguing blend of songs. There is Pat Boone's version of 'Crazy Train' (the aging crooner was a one-time Osbourne neighbour); The Kinks' 'You Really Got Me'; songs by Starsailor, The Cars, John Lennon and System Of A Down; and several of Ozzy's favourites, including 'Mama, I'm Coming Home' and 'Dreamer'.

Meanwhile, Kelly cut a music video with Los Angeles videographer Marcus Siega and made her first ever public appearance at the KIIS-FM (a major California radio station) Wango Tango concert on 15 June.

In a recent conversation with another media outlet, Ozzy talked about the success he has enjoyed, his continuing attraction and what makes him happy. "I'm 53 and I'm getting more work than ever," he replied. "The American leg of the Ozzfest sold out within an hour. Last week I got a star on the Hollywood Walk of Fame [the legendary street of dreams where everyone from Marilyn Monroe to...well...Ozzy Osbourne is given a small dedication plaque embedded in the sidewalk cement]. I've got a hit television programme and every week it's getting higher ratings. And I'm really happy for Sharon,* because she's been my other half for 20 years and she's finally gotten some recognition. [And] I think [the kids] are handling it a lot better than I would have at their age. At 16, 17, if you put me in their position, my head would've been bigger than Sunset Boulevard.

---

* Sharon was recognised some years back when Ozzy, in a fit of rage and a vodka frenzy, tried to strangle his better half.

"I think what's kept me sane all these years – or as sane as I can be; I'm far from sane – is that I love my dogs, my kids, my wife, my house. So am I going to sit there with the dog turds, going, 'What time does the maid come in?'* [The show] hasn't changed my marriage. I loved my wife before this show and I love her now. To see my wife and children happy, that's all that matters to me."

Fair enough. Not many artists make the jump from musician to bigger-than-life figure. The *National Enquirer* now regularly goes dumpster-diving through his trash and revered long-running news show *60 Minutes* is calling him for a segment. Mike Myers, the *Saturday Night Live* alumnus who first gained real fame with his *Wayne's World* send-ups, even made a visit to the Osbourne manse to ask the family if they would make a cameo appearance in his third and newest Austin Powers spy spoof, *Austin Powers: Goldmember*. The family agreed, and before the film's release, one can only surmise that whatever they did was wild and groovy.

Beyond the histrionics – or, more precisely, behind them – is the simple fact that Ozzy Osbourne, Prince of Darkness, TV heartthrob, political kingpin and, oh yes, singer, is a very, very nice man. He mumbles, shuffles and strays from conversational topics, but he is as sweet a person that has ever beheaded a winged creature. I've met him many times and he has never failed to be polite (beyond the bar-room brogue),

---

* In an episode of the show, Ozzy does the devil's business himself and retrieves a dropping from a hardwood floor.

interested in what you're saying and honest to the point of embarrassment. When I sat down to speak with him in 2002, he was talking about his leg and stomach troubles, how he felt like there were weights hanging from his balls, yada yada, and the entire conversation came off with a deadpan delivery. Ozzy is a laugh riot, yet he really has no idea how funny he is. He never relates a tale to elicit sympathy. Rather, he just lets the adjectives roll and only when he's hit a particularly funny moment will he allow himself a grin, much less a minor chuckle.

So what we see when we witness Ozzy on television picking up dog crap or lecturing his daughter on the "vagina police" or telling his son about the dangers of alcohol and other substances is simply Ozzy being Ozzy. It's not there for effect, not there for a laugh; it's there for no other reason than he is the man he is and these are the words he'd be relating whether ten cameras were focused on him or not.

And he's never changed. When we first met, on a Black Sabbath tour nearly 30 years ago, he was so whacked on booze and coke and pills that he could barely talk, but God, was he funny and polite. Just minutes before he was due to go on stage, he was sitting there with a punk journalist holding a $20 tape player and telling me about the albums and the music and England and what the deal was. He was dressed in black (his colour of choice), his jailhouse tats visible as he lifted his hands to make a point. He could see I was visibly nervous, and I was – in fact, I was freaking terrified – but he was so genteel. Speech slurred, barely able to lift himself from the bed to make his way to the arena, he answered every question with as much thought and insight as he could muster. To this day, I've never forgotten the way he treated me, not so much as a professional but just as an equal, a kid in love with a band called Black Sabbath. At 27 or 57, Ozzy O has never changed.

And perhaps the one thing that has never changed in his life is his love for Paul McCartney. He recently played with Paul on a bill at the Queen's Party, a monster show staged in celebration of the Queen's Golden Jubilee and MC'd by Sharon. Upon leaving the stage, the singer bade the crowd an adieu with 'God Save the Queen'. Ozzy actually met the Beatle in the previous year on *The Howard Stern Show*, the talk show whose controversial host has virtually ruled the radio waves these last several years. In fact, Howard maintains that it was his idea to do a quasi-reality show with the Osbournes when he invited them to appear on one of his shows.

"I met my hero, Paul McCartney, last year at *The Howard Stern Show*," Ozzy related to a guitar magazine, "and there were photographs taken of me and him, and I wrote to him and asked if I could have one. He never got back to me, and I was kind of disappointed. I mean, The Beatles were the reason I wanted to get into music. I wanted Paul to play on 'Dreamer' [from the *Down To Earth* album], but he didn't want to do it. He said, 'I couldn't play it any better than the bass player that's already playing on there.' But that wasn't the point; the point was to have

Paul McCartney playing bass on one of the most Beatles-esque songs I've ever written. He apologised to me and I told him to forget it. Just the fact that he'd sat down and listened to my song was enough for me."

Reading between the lines, it seems that Paul was maybe not entirely thrilled with the idea of playing bass for Mr O, but then again he may just have been busy. In any case, the new album has been selling extraordinarily well and the life of Ozzy reads like a fairy tale. What will be interesting is watching the Osbourne brood growing up over the next several years and seeing how they handle having the world handed to them. And there's probably only one way to know that – to watch the second season of *The Osbournes*.

Author's Outsight

On these pages, I have tried to portray this animal known as Black Sabbath – at times a tiger and at times a tabby – as honestly and as neutrally as possible. Like you, I have my favourite songs, those special tunes that bring you back or propel you forward, etched in your mind with a diamond needle. I've tried to capture the foibles, follies, lunatic antics and, most importantly, the interactions among the band.

From the outset, I stressed that this book would not dwell on the demented or focus on the fantastic. I mean, hell, does it intrigue you if I told you that Tony met his wife at the Rainbow in Hollywood, a club/restaurant that has been a mainstay of visiting rock musicians? Or that once, when Tony phoned Lita in her hotel room, Billy Sheehan answered the phone? Or the fact that John Downing was murdered a couple years after his altercation with Glenn Hughes? Or the fact that Tony was downing Halcyons and Xanaxes like M&Ms?

Well, I must admit, there is a bit of that accident-at-the-side-of-the-road mentality here – you just have to stop and look. So let's stop for a minute and listen to a close friend of Tony's unveil a more personal side: "He was a rock star, and it's lonely being in a hotel by yourself. He liked to have people around. And he wouldn't listen to any contemporary music. He wouldn't listen to Alice In Chains or Soundgarden; he listened to Frank Sinatra. He never really liked listening to popular music. He thought it was terrible."

Here is another unbelievable but 100 per cent true story: "I was with Tony and this package sent to him starts to stink. Now, they got some weird shit in the mail, so I opened up this thing and it was a letter written in blood. It almost gave me a heart attack. That was gross. It was a fork and knife and a note, and it said, 'You'll have to eat shit before you ever have a hit record again, love Sharon and Ozzy.' [Sharon] had emptied their kids' diapers into this bag. That's the kind of bullshit that was going on."

And here's a little ditty about Tony and Lita: "I was about 22 and I was with Tony. I went over to his house to visit and sometimes I couldn't wake him up because he'd be sleeping. He got in a fight with Lita once and he had drunk a bottle of Jack Daniel's and God knows what else, and I was, like, 'Wake up! Wake up!' It totally freaked me out. And then I started pounding on him, jumping. I'm pulling his hair and I couldn't get him to budge. And finally, this big hand comes out and is smacking me, and it was, like, 'Thank God! He's alive.'"

Fetishes? "I never saw a Satanic Bible. I never even saw a candle in his room, except I had to buy him underwear and socks, and it had to be black, and trying to find Fruit Of The Loom three-packs in black isn't easy. And he would get paranoid. Once, he said, 'Someone is stealing my underpants and socks.' And I'm like, 'What are you talking about? You're crazy.' And he'd go, 'No. The maid or somebody is coming in the room and stealing my socks and underpants.' And I went, 'You are nuts. They don't want your smelly socks.' And when I cleaned his room, in the very back in the closet under all this crap, all wadded up, would be black underwear and socks."

Okay, so I succumbed. But that isn't the main intent of this book in any way. Black Sabbath has been an integral and crucial part of the development of rock since they started the headbanging craze 25-plus years ago. They even attempted another reunion in around 1994 and actually performed at one show in Costa Mesa, California, but this was really little more than an abortion gone bad.* You

* Prior to this closing gig in Costa Mesa, the band had been talking on a virtually daily basis for eight months prior. It began as a two-month tour, then an album, then an additional live album, and by the time conversations had ceased (they never once located themselves in the same room) plans had them working together for an entire year. "But Ozzy's side changed their minds," remembers Tony Iommi. "They got too greedy. I think they wanted too much money, something in the range of $20 million. Because we enjoyed it when we all played together on that reunion show. That was Ozzy's final gig [of that tour], and that's how we broke up with Dio, because Dio wouldn't do this. He refused to go on stage 'with the clown', were his words. So Rob Halford called us and we rehearsed a day with Rob – he knew the old songs – and we went on and played a set with Bill, Geezer, Rob Halford and Geoff [Nicholls]. And then, the second day of that show, we did a reunion with Ozzy. Four numbers. It was great! That's when we really started talking about putting the band back together. But then there were lies involved, management, four different record companies, four managements – four liars – and umpteen other things. It got silly. And, even though we said yes, [Osbourne's people] didn't want to do it again. Ozzy wasn't ready to do it.

"The purpose of the thing was a nice idea – we could have earned a lot of money and we could have had a great time, if we could have just let it go at that – but then you start wanting this and that. It just got out of hand and fell apart. I feel sorry for Bill Ward, because he was doing a solo album at the time [Ward I] and he just stopped the project altogether and put it on the shelf for eight months. Bill concentrated on the Sabbath thing. That's all he thought about, getting his drum risers built and finding people to build his kit, doing this and that, and of course it was devastating when he heard it wasn't going to happen, so he had to pick up the pieces. I just carried on and went on to make an album. And now? Geezer's with Ozzy again! After all that time saying he would never go back with Ozzy, he's with Ozzy.

"The way I look at it is that, if some people can't work the way you want them, bring in somebody else. There are times on the past albums when they'd be gone all day and leave me in the studio. They'd all be off in the fucking Bahamas somewhere and I'd be in London, in a dark studio, mixing the albums day and night. The original line-up got to the stage where we were never doing anything. They'd all go away on holidays when I was in the studio. It was a bloody nightmare, in a lot of cases, and the original line-up wasn't necessarily the most satisfying, because there were always problems. There was always something going on. And those eight months of trying to put the band back together showed it was no different. It's still got problems and aggravation."

can't go home. The bridge is burned, and though the light may be shining from one end of the tunnel, any attempt to turn around and return whence you came will most probably result in running head-on into an oncoming train.

Take them into your heart and balance their music against what has come since. An intriguing thought is, what if these four players met today? Would they find mutual release in music? Could they even be friends? Bill Ward helps us with the answer and draws this tale to a close: "Would we be friends? Good question. Partially, yeah, to the point where I felt relatively safe within myself. A lot of things that I was attracted to I no longer need in my life. Ozzy's insanity. Geezer. I haven't talked or had a conversation with him in many, many years. And Tony. I feel I was having some really nice conversations with him last year, and I could probably still hang with Tony. I could probably still hang with all of them. But let's look at reality for a second, because my association with them is minimal. So maybe that answers the question right there. Will I be talking to Tony? No.

"However, I must point out that, if I needed to call them for any reason, any three of them, then I would. If they responded, that's fine, but I would always reach out to them. And any one of them can reach out to me, day or night, and I will always be there to try and be as helpful as I can, as a friend. So that remains in position. My loyalty and friendship still exists there.

"Also, I pray for Tony, Ozzy and Geez. I pray for them every single day. I have done for about eleven years, and I don't miss a day. There's still a lot of love there."

Discography

18 September 1970
Paranoid
Vertigo 6360 011
'War Pigs' / 'Paranoid' / 'Planet Caravan' / 'Iron Man' /
'Electric Funeral' / 'Hand Of Doom' / 'Rat Salad' / 'Fairies
Wear Boots'

December 1973 (reissue)
Paranoid
WWA 007

January 1976 (reissue)
Paranoid
NEMS NEL 6003
WS 1887
(Also on Italian Vertigo / American WB)

1986 (reissue on CD)
Paranoid
Castle CLACD 197

August 1971
Master Of Reality
Vertigo 6360 050
'Sweet Leaf' / 'After Forever' / 'Embryo' / 'Children Of The
Grave' / 'Orchid' / 'Lord Of This World' / 'Solitude' / 'Into
The Void'

December 1973 (reissue)
Master Of Reality
WWA 008

February 1976 (reissue)
Master Of Reality
NEMS NEL 6004
(Also on Dutch NEMS)

1986 (reissue on CD)
Master Of Reality
Castle CLACD 198

September 1972
Black Sabbath Volume 4
Vertigo 6360 071
'Wheels Of Confusion' / 'Tomorrow's Dream' / 'Changes' / 'FX' / 'Supernaut' / 'Snowblind' / 'Cornucopia' / 'Laguna Sunrise' / 'St Vitus Dance' / 'Under The Sun'

December 1973 (reissue)
Black Sabbath Volume 4
WWA 009

February 1976 (reissue)
Black Sabbath Volume 4
NEMS NEL 6005

1986 (reissue on CD)
Black Sabbath Volume 4
Castle CLACD 199

November 1973
Sabbath Bloody Sabbath
WWA 005

'Sabbath Bloody Sabbath' / 'A National Acrobat' / 'Fluff'
/ 'Sabbra Cadabra' / 'Killing Yourself To Live' / 'Who
Are You' / 'Looking For Today' / 'Spiral Architect'

June 1980 (reissue)
Sabbath Bloody Sabbath
NEMS NEL 6017
BS 2695
(Also on Canadian WB)

1986 (reissue on CD)
Sabbath Bloody Sabbath
Castle CLACD 201
(All above LPs above moved to WWA in December 1973)

September 1975
Sabotage
NEMS 9199 001
'Am I Going Insane (Radio)' / 'Hole In The Sky' / 'Don't
Start (Too Late)' / 'Symptom Of The Universe' /
'Megalomania' / 'The Writ' / 'Supertzar' / 'Thrill Of It All'

June 1980 (reissue)
Sabotage
NEMS NEL 6018
BS 2822
(Also on American WB)

1986 (reissue on CD)
Sabotage
Castle CLACD 202

December 1975
We Sold Our Soul For Rock 'n' Roll (double album)
NEMS 6641 335
'Am I Going Insane (Radio)' / 'Black Sabbath' / 'Changes'
/ 'Children Of The Grave' / 'Fairies Wear Boots' / 'Iron
Man' / 'Laguna Sunrise' / 'NIB' / 'Paranoid' / 'Sabbath
Bloody Sabbath' / 'Snowblind' / 'Sweet Leaf' / 'Tomorrow's
Dream' / 'War Pigs' / 'Warning' / 'Wicked World' / 'The
Wizard'

August 1976 (reissue)
We Sold Our Soul For Rock 'n' Roll
NEMS NELD 101

October 1976
Technical Ecstasy
Vertigo 9102 750
'Back Street Kids' / 'You Won't Change Me' / 'Rock 'n'
Roll Doctor' / 'It's Alright' / 'All Moving Parts (Stand
Still)' / 'She's Gone' / 'Dirty Women' / 'Gypsy'

1996 (reissue on CD)
Technical Ecstasy
ESM CD 328

December 1977
Greatest Hits
NEMS NEL 6009
'Paranoid' / 'NIB' / 'Changes' / 'Sabbath Bloody Sabbath'
/ 'War Pigs' / 'Laguna Sunrise' / 'Tomorrow's Dream' /
'Sweet Leaf'

1986 (reissue)
Greatest Hits
Castle CLACD 200
(Includes extra track, 'After Forever')

October 1978
Never Say Die
Vertigo 9102 751
'Swinging The Chain' / 'Never Say Die' / 'Hard Road' /
'Shock Wave' / 'Johnny Blade' / 'Junior's Eyes' / 'Air
Dance' / 'Break Out' / 'Over To You'

September 1993 (reissue)
Never Say Die
Spectrum

1996 (reissue on CD)
Never Say Die
ESM CD 329
April 1980
Heaven And Hell
Vertigo 9102 752
'Lonely Is The Word' / 'Heaven And Hell' / 'Children Of
The Sea' / 'Wishing Well' / 'Lady Evil' / 'Neon Knights' /
'Die Young' / 'Walk Away'

May 1983 (reissue on CD)
Heaven And Hell
Spectrum

1996 (reissue on CD)

Heaven And Hell
ESM CD 330

June 1980
Black Sabbath Live At Last
NEMS BS 001 (Released after to a ten-year dispute between band and former manager)
'Tomorrow's Dream' / 'Sweet Leaf' / 'Killing Yourself To Live' / 'Cornucopia' / 'Snowblind' / 'Children Of The Grave' / 'War Pigs' / 'Wicked World' / 'Paranoid'

November 1981
Mob Rules
Vertigo 6302 119
'The Sign Of The Southern Cross' / 'Mob Rules' / 'Slipping Away' / 'Turn Up The Night' / 'Voodoo' / 'Country Girl' / 'Over And Over' / 'Falling Off The Edge Of The World' / 'E5150'

1996 (reissue on CD)
Mob Rules
ESM CD 332

January 1983
Live Evil
Vertigo SAB 10
'Children Of The Sea' / 'Black Sabbath' / 'Paranoid' / 'Neon Knights' / 'Iron Man' / 'Children Of The Grave' / 'E5150' / 'Heaven And Hell' / 'Voodoo' / 'Sign Of The Southern Cross' / 'War Pigs' / 'Mob Rules' / 'Fluff' / 'NIB'

September 1983
Born Again
Vertigo VERL 8
'Disturbing The Priest' / 'Stonehenge' / 'Zero The Hero' /
'Trashed' / 'The Dark' / 'Born Again' / 'Hot Line' / 'Digital
Bitch' / 'Keep It Warm'

March 1986
Seventh Star: Black Sabbath Featuring Tony Iommi
Vertigo VERH 29
'In For The Kill' / 'No Stranger To Love' / 'Heart Like A
Wheel' / 'Sphinx (The Guardian)' / 'Turn To Stone' /
'Angry Heart' / 'Danger' / 'Seventh Star' / 'In Memory'

November 1987
The Eternal Idol
Vertigo VERH 51
'The Shining' / 'Ancient Warrior' / 'Born To Lose' / 'Lost
Forever' / 'Hard Life To Love' / 'Scarlet Pimpernel' /
'Glory Ride' / 'Eternal Idol'

April 1989
Headless Cross
IRS EIRSA 1002
'Gates To Hell' / 'Headless Cross' / 'Devil And Daughter'
/ 'When Death Calls' / 'Kick In The Spirit World' / 'Call
Of The Wild' / 'Black Moon' / 'Night'

August 1990
TYR
IRS EIRSA 1038

'Anno Mundi' / 'The Lawmaker' / 'Jerusalem' / 'The Sabbath Stones' / 'The Battle Of TYR' / 'Odin's Court' / 'Valhalla' / 'Feels Good To Me' / 'Heaven In Black'

June 1992
Dehumanizer
IRS EIRSCD 1064
'Computer God' / 'After All (The Dead)' / 'TV Crimes' / 'Letters From Earth' / 'Masters Of Insanity' / 'Time Machine' / 'Sins Of The Father' / 'Too Late' / '1' / 'Buried Alive'

February 1994
Cross Purposes
'I Witness' / 'Cross Of Thorns' / 'Psychophobia' / 'Virtual Death' / 'Immaculate Deception' / 'Dying For Love' / 'Back To Eden' / 'The Hand That Rocks The Cradle' / 'Cardinal Sin' / 'Evil Eye'

September 1995
Forbidden
'Forbidden' / 'Get A Grip' / 'Can't Get Close Enough' / 'Shakin' Off The Chains' / 'I Won't Cry For You' / 'The Illusion Of Power' / 'Kiss Of Death' / 'Rusty Angels' / 'Sick And Tired' / 'Guilty As Hell'

October 1998
Reunion (double album)
'War Pigs' / 'Behind The Wall Of Sleep' / 'NIB' / 'Fairies Wear Boots' / 'Electric Funeral' / 'Sweet Leaf' / 'Spiral Architect' / 'Into The Void' / 'Snowblind' // 'Sabbath

Bloody Sabbath' / 'Orchid / Lord Of This World' / 'Dirty Women' / 'Black Sabbath' / 'Iron Man' / 'Children Of The Grave' / 'Paranoid' / 'Psycho Man' / 'Selling My Soul'

UK SINGLES

Circa 1969
'Song For Jim'

Circa 1969
'The Rebel' (demo)

January 1970
'Evil Woman (Don't Play Your Games With Me)' / 'Wicked World'
Fontana TF 1067

March 1970 (reissue)
'Evil Woman (Don't Play Your Games With Me)' / 'Wicked World'
Vertigo V2

August 1970
'Paranoid' / 'The Wizard'
Vertigo 6059 010

January 1972
'Iron Man' / 'Electric Funeral'

September 1972

'Tomorrow's Dream' / 'Laguna Sunrise'
Vertigo 6059 061

October 1973
'Sabbath Bloody Sabbath' / 'Changes'
WWA WWS 002

February 1976
'Am I Going Insane (Radio)' / 'Hole In The Sky'
NEMS 6165 300

February 1977 (reissue)
'Paranoid' / 'Snowblind'
NEMS NES 112

November 1976
'It's Alright' / 'Rock 'n' Roll Doctor'
(Never charted)

June 1978
'Never Say Die' / 'She's Gone'
Vertigo SAB 1

October 1978
'Hard Road' / 'Symptom Of The Universe'
Vertigo SAB 2
(Also released on purple vinyl)

June 1980
'Neon Knights' / 'Children Of The Sea (Live)'
Vertigo SAB 3

June 1980 (reissue)
'Paranoid' / 'Snowblind'
NEMS BSS 101

November 1980
'Die Young' / 'Heaven And Hell'
Vertigo SAB 4

November 1980
'Die Young' / 'Heaven And Hell' (live twelve-inch)
Vertigo SAB 412

October 1981
'Mob Rules' / 'Die Young'
Vertigo SAB 5

October 1981
'Mob Rules' / 'Die Young'
Vertigo SAB 512

February 1982
'Turn Up The Night' / 'Lonely Is The Word' (picture disc)
Vertigo SAB 6

February 1982
'Turn Up The Night' / 'Lonely Is The Word' (twelve-inch picture disc)
Vertigo SABP 612

October 1983
'Stonehenge' / 'Thrashed'

June 1989
'Devil And Daughter' / 15-Minute Interview

September 1990
'Feels Good To Me' / 'Paranoid' (live)

June 1992
'TV Crimes' / 'Letters From Earth'
IRS EIRSP 178

US ALBUMS

Tracks will be listed only if different from UK releases

1970
Black Sabbath
WB 1871-2
'Black Sabbath' / 'The Wizard' / 'Wasp' / 'Behind The
Wall Of Sleep' / 'Basically' / 'NIB' / 'Wicked World' / 'A
Bit Of Finger' / 'Sleeping Village' / 'Warning'

1971
Paranoid
WB 3104-2

1971
Master Of Reality
WB 2562-2

1972
Black Sabbath Volume 4

WB 2602-2

1974
Sabbath Bloody Sabbath
WB 2695-2

1975
Sabotage
WB 2822-2

1976
We Sold Our Soul For Rock 'n' Roll
WB 2923-2

1976
Technical Ecstasy
WB 2969-2

1978
Never Say Die
WB 3186-2

1980
Heaven And Hell
WB 3372-2

1981
Mob Rules
WB 3605-2

1982

Live Evil
WB 9 23742-2

1983
Born Again

1986
Seventh Star: Black Sabbath Featuring Tony Iommi

1987
Eternal Idol
WB 9 25548-2

1989
Headless Cross
IRS X2 0777 2
13002 2 6

1990
TYR
IRS X2 13049

1992
Dehumanizer
Reprise 9 26965-2
(*Wayne's World* version available on CD only)

1994
Cross Purposes
IRS 07777 13222 2 8

1995
Forbidden
IRS 72438 3062027

1998
Reunion

US SINGLES (ON AMERICAN WB)

Circa 1969
'Song For Jim'

Circa 1969
'The Rebel' (demo)

January 1970
'Evil Woman (Don't Play Your Games With Me)' / 'Wicked World'

March 1970 (reissue)
'Evil Woman (Don't Play Your Games With Me)' / 'Wicked World'

August 1970
'Paranoid' / 'The Wizard'

January 1972
'Iron Man' / 'Electric Funeral'

September 1972
'Tomorrow's Dream' / 'Laguna Sunrise'

October 1973
'Sabbath Bloody Sabbath' / 'Changes'

February 1976
'Am I Going Insane (Radio)' / 'Hole in The Sky'

November 1976
'It's Alright' / 'Rock 'n' Roll Doctor'
(Never charted)

February 1977 (reissue)
'Paranoid' / 'Snowblind'

June 1978
'Never Say Die' / 'She's Gone'

October 1978
'Hard Road' / 'Symptom Of The Universe'
(Also released on purple vinyl)

June 1980
'Neon Knights' / 'Children Of The Sea (Live)'

June 1980 (reissue)
'Paranoid' / 'Snowblind'

November 1980
'Die Young' / 'Heaven And Hell'

November 1980
'Die Young' / 'Heaven And Hell' (live twelve-inch)

October 1981
'Mob Rules' / 'Die Young'

October 1981
'Mob Rules' / 'Die Young' (twelve-inch)

February 1982
'Turn Up The Night' / 'Lonely Is The Word' (picture disc)

February 1982
'Turn Up The Night' / 'Lonely Is The Word' (twelve-inch picture disc)

October 1983
'Stonehenge' / 'Thrashed'

June 1989
'Devil And Daughter' / 15-Minute Interview

September 1990
'Feels Good To Me' / 'Paranoid (Live)'

June 1992
'TV Crimes' / 'Letters From Earth'

BOOTLEG ALBUMS

1970 – Berlin, Germany
Return to 1969

1970 – Paris, France

War Pigs

1970 – San Francisco (Beat Club), US
Black Nights

1971 – Toronto, Canada
Wicked Sabbath

1973
Love In Chicago
Berkeley 2049 / 2050 (mono)
'Sweet Leaf' / 'Killing Yourself To Live' / 'Tomorrow's
Dream' / 'Snowblind' / 'Sabbra Cadabra' / 'What To Do'
/ 'Supernaut' / 'Iron Man' / 'Black Sabbath' / 'Children
Of The Grave' / 'War Pigs' / 'Paranoid'

1974 – California Jam, US
Bagdad

Recorded during 1975 US tour
Grindlepol
TAKRL 1379
'Killing Yourself To Live' / 'Hole In The Sky' / 'Snowblind'
/ 'Killing Yourself To Live (2)' / 'War Pigs' / 'Children Of
The Grave'

1975 / 1978 – USA / UK
Symptom Of The Paranoid (double CD)

Recorded at US halls / concerts in 1975 and 1978
Unorthodox

Impossible Recordworks IMP 1-29
'Snowblind' / 'Black Sabbath' / 'Iron Man' / 'Paranoid'
/ 'Killing Yourself To Live' / 'Hole In The Sky' / 'War
Pigs'

1977 – Lund, Sweden
Killing Yourself To Die

21 April 1977
Killing Yourself To Die (double album)
Stone Records 4
'Supertzar' / 'Symptom Of The Universe' / 'Snowblind' /
'War Pigs' / 'Black Sabbath' / Medley: 'Dirty Women';
drum solo; 'Rock 'n' Roll Doctor' / Medley: guitar solo,
improvisation / 'Electric Funeral; guitar solo' / 'NIB' /
'Gypsy' / 'Paranoid' / 'Children Of The Grave'

1978 – Fresno, US
One For The Nose

1978 – London, UK
Welcome To The Electric Funeral

The 1978 American Tour
6144 (mono)
'Black Sabbath' / 'Iron Man' / 'Paranoid' / 'Symptom Of
The Universe' / 'War Pigs' / 'Gypsy' / 'Children Of The
Grave'

1980 – Seattle, US
Dance Of The Devil

1980 – Tokyo, Japan
Sabbath Day's Journey

1980 – Tokyo, Japan
Angel And Demon

1980 – Sydney, Australia
Burning The Cross

1980 – New York, US
Heavenly Hell (double CD)

1980 – Miami, US
Miami '80 (double CD)

17 August 1980
Death Riders / Their Satanic Majesties
Witch Records LSD-666-WRS80-3
'War Pigs' / 'Neon Knights' / 'Heaven And Hell' / 'NIB' /
'Iron Man' / 'Die Young' / 'Paranoid'

Doomsday Recitation (stereo)
Impossible Recordworks
(Same tracks as *Killing Yourself To Die*)
Recorded during 1978 US tour

20 January 1981
London Hammersmith Odeon (double album)
BM0 8101 A / B / C / D
'Supertzar' / 'War Pigs' / 'Neon Knights' / 'NIB' / 'Children
Of The Sea' / 'Sweet Leaf' / 'Lady Evil' / 'Black Sabbath'

/ 'Heaven And Hell' / 'Iron Man' / 'Die Young' / 'Paranoid'
/ 'Children Of The Grave'

1981 Japan
Nuclear Poisoner
'Neon Knights' / 'NIB' / 'Children Of The Sea' / 'Sweet
Leaf' / 'Black Sabbath' / 'Heaven And Hell' / 'Iron Man'

1981 – London / 1983 – Reading, UK
Live Murder Act I / Act II (double CD)

1983 – Reading Festival, UK
Smoke On The Water (double CD)

1983 – Chicago / Reading Festival, US / UK
Chicago '83 (double CD)

1983 – Paris, France
Parisian Bitch

1983 – Quebec, Canada
Black And Purple (double CD)

1986 – Hollywood, US
Turn To Glenn

1986 / 87 – Texas, US
The Ray Gillen Years (studio)

1986 – London, UK
Ray Rules

1987 – Bremen, Germany
Eternal Shining

1989 – Manchester, UK
Death Called '89

1992 – Emilio, Italy (Reggio)
Reviviscence!

1992 – Emilio, Italy (Reggio)
Europe 1993

1992 – Boston, US
As Darkness Hits (double CD)

1992 – Heidelberg, Germany
Tony Martin And Friends

1992 – Costa Mesa, US
Ozzy Osbourne – Final Concert (triple CD)

1992 – Costa Mesa, US
Ozzy Meets The Priest

1992 / 94
Iron Men (double CD)

1995 – Karlshamn, Sweden
Beast In Heaven

1995 – UK

Live In The UK (double CD)

1996 – UK
Eighth Star (studio)

1985 – Live Aid / 1997 – Ozzfest
The Zakkman Cometh (double CD)

1998 – Budapest, Hungary
Ozzy Rules Budapest

Various recordings
The Archangel Rides Again

BOOTLEG TAPES

1970 – Germany (C60)
(The version of 'War Pigs' that appears on this tape has different lyrics)

1971 – Paris, France

October 1972 – Hollywood Bowl, California, USA

March 1973 – Greens Playhouse, Glasgow, Scotland (C90)

1974 – California, US
California Jam

1975 – Santa Monica, California, USA

1975 – Colston Hall, Bristol, UK (C120)

October 1975 – Lewisham Odeon, London, UK (C90)

21 November 1975 – Gaumont State Theatre, Kilburn, UK

22 November 1975 – Capitol Theatre, Cardiff, Wales (C90)

January 1977 – London, UK (C60)

12 March 1977 – Hammersmith Odeon, London, UK (C90)

13 March 1977 – Hammersmith Odeon, London, UK
1978 – Hammersmith Odeon, London, UK (C90)

1978 – Newcastle, UK

1978 – Italy

18 May 1978 – Apollo, Glasgow, Scotland (C90)

19 June 1978
Megaton Surprise
Hammersmith Odeon, London, UK (C90)

17 September 1978 – Pittsburgh, USA (C60)

1980 – Southampton, UK

23 May 1980 – Apollo, Manchester, UK (C90)

20 January 1981 – Hammersmith Odeon, London, UK

6 January 1982 – City Hall, Newcastle, UK (C90)

BOOTLEG VIDEOTAPES

1978 – Hammersmith Odeon, London, UK
'Supertzar' / 'Symptom Of The Universe' / 'War Pigs' /
'Snowblind' / 'Never Say Die' / 'Black Sabbath' / 'Dirty
Women' / 'Rock 'n' Roll Doctor' / 'Electric Funeral' /
'Children Of The Grave' / 'Paranoid'

1997 – Birmingham, UK
The Last Supper (DVD)

We Sold Our Souls For Rock 'n' Roll (Penelope Spheeris
documentary)

April 1996
Cross Purposes Live
CD IRS 7243 4 77806 08

FORMER MEMBERS' INDIVIDUAL PROJECTS

OZZY OSBOURNE

September 1980
Blizzard Of Ozz
Epic EK 67235

October 1981
Diary Of A Madman
Epic EK 67236

November 1982
Speak Of The Devil
Epic EK 67237

December 1983
Bark At The Moon
Epic EK 67238

February 1986
The Ultimate Sin
Epic EK 67239

May 1987
Tribute
Epic EK 67240

October 1988
No Rest For The Wicked
Epic EK 67241

March 1990
Just Say Ozzy
Epic EK 67242

October 1991
No More Tears
Epic EK 67243

June 1993
Live & Loud
Epic E2K 67244

October 1995
Ozzmosis
Epic EK 67091

2000
Down To Earth

GEEZER BUTLER

1995
Plastic Planet (as g//z/r)
TVT 6010-2

1 July 1997
Black Science
CD TVT TVT6020-2

BILL WARD

1990
Ward I (features 'Along The Way' with Jack Bruce, Zakk
Wylde, Lanny Cordola and Ozzy)
Chameleon

1996
When The Bough Breaks

2001
Beyond Aston
(original title: *Remembering*)

RONNIE DIO

June 1983
Holy Diver
Reprise

July 1984
The Last In Line
WB

August 1985
Sacred Heart
WB

June 1986
Intermission
WB

August 1987
Dream Evil
WB

May 1990
Lock Up The Wolves
WB

March 1992

Diamonds – The Best Of Dio
WB

October 1993
Strange Highways

23 September 1996
Angry Machines
CD CBH / Steamhammer 085-18292
Futurist

24 February 1998
Inferno: The Last In Live
Futurist

2 March 2000
Magica
Spitfire 6-70211-5020-2

3 October 2000
The Very Best Of Dio

COMPILATIONS, TRIBUTES AND MISCELLANEOUS

August 1985
The Collection
Castle

December 1985
Boxed set – first six LPs plus *Live At Last*

June 1986
Classic Cuts From The Vaults
Archive 4

November 1989
Blackest Sabbath

June 1990
Backtrackin'

May 1991
The Ozzy Osbourne Years (the first six albums)
Castle ESB CD 142

1991
Between Heaven And Hell
Castle RAW CD 104

Axe Attack Volume 2 (contains 'Die Young')
K-Tel

Heavy Metal (contains 'Mob Rules')

Radio Active (contains 'Paranoid')

Live And Heavy (contains 'Paranoid')
NEMS NEL 6020

Heavy Rock (contains 'Die Young' / 'Heaven And Hell')

Double Hard (contains 'Paranoid [Live]')

1994
Nativity In Black: A Tribute To Black Sabbath*
Col CK 66335

Second Stage Live (contains tracks lifted from Ozzfest
in 1996 and 2000)

IMPORT ALBUMS

The Original Black Sabbath
NEMS (German import)
'NIB' / 'War Pigs' / 'Changes' / 'Tomorrow's Dream'

1978
Best Vibrations
NEMS ZNLNE 33116 (Italian import)
'Black Sabbath' / 'The Wizard' / 'Warning' / 'Paranoid' /
'War Pigs' / 'Iron Man' / 'Wicked World'

Star Gold (double album)
NEMS (German import)
(Includes most tracks from the import *We Sold Our Soul
For Rock 'n Roll* plus the bonus track 'Solitude')

Rock Legends
Vertigo 8321 120 (Australian import)
'Backstreet Kids' / 'Rock 'n' Roll Doctor' / 'Dirty Women' /
'Never Say Die' / 'Shock Wave' / 'Air Dance' / 'Johnny Blade'

---

* Under the tag The Bullring Brummies, Butler and Ward actually performed together on
one track, 'The Wizard'. Tony was originally meant to play on the song (he's not listed in
the credits), but after the tapes were sent to him in London (the album was recorded at
Conway Studios in Los Angeles) he wasn't happy with what he heard.

Starburst (double import)

MISCELLANEOUS VIDEOS

1991
The Black Sabbath Story: Volume 1 (1970-1978)
Castle 38316-3
'NIB' / 'Paranoid' / 'War Pigs' / 'Children Of The Grave'
/ 'Snowblind' / 'Sabbath Bloody Sabbath' / 'Symptom Of
The Universe' / 'It's Alright' / 'Rock 'n' Roll Doctor' /
'Never Say Die'

1992
The Black Sabbath Story: Volume 2 (1978-1992)
Castle 38333-3
'A Hard Road' / 'Die Young' / 'Neon Knights' / 'Trashed'
/ 'Zero The Hero' / 'No Stranger To Love' / 'The Shining'
/ 'Headless Cross' / 'Feels Good To Me' / 'TV Crimes' /
'Computer God' / '1'

Live & Loud
Epic 29V49151

Don't Blame Me
SMU Ent 19V-49103

The Ultimate Ozzy
CBS Fox 6199

Wicked Videos
49008

1995
Plastic Planet (Promo video for Butler's Plastic Planet
CD, seven minutes and 35 seconds long)
EPK* *TRT-TVT Records

Bibliography

Jones, Peter and Jasper, Tony: *20 Years Of British Record Charts* (Queen Anne Press Ltd, 1955-75)

Paraire, Philippe: 50 Years Of Rock Music (Chambers)

McAleer, Dave: *The All Music Book Of Hit Singles* (Miller Freeman Books, 1994)

Erlewine, Michael; Bogdanov, Vladimir; and Woodstra, Chris: *The All Music Guide To Rock* (Miller Freeman Books, 1995)

Erlewine, Michael; Bogdanov, Vladimir; and Woodstra, Chris: *The All Music Guide To Rock* (second edition, Miller Freeman Books)

Kline, Gerry and Jacobs, Jack: *Black Sabbath Rock-It Comix* (Rock-It Comix, February 1994)

Marsh, Dave and Dell, Kevin Stein: *The Book Of Rock Lists* (*Rolling Stone* Press Book, 1981)

The Book Of Rock Lists includes Black Sabbath under "Beyond
Plutonium: 15 Great Heavy Metal Bands"

1   Blue Öyster Cult
2   Led Zeppelin
3   Van Halen
4   Black Sabbath
5   Thin Lizzy
6   Deep Purple
7   Ted Nugent And The (latter-day) Amboy Dukes
8   Aerosmith
9   Grand Funk Railroad
10 Dust
11 Blue Cheer
12 Sir Lord Baltimore
13 AC/DC
14 Iron Butterfly
15 Uriah Heep

Schaffner, Nicholas: *The British Invasion* (McGraw-Hill)

Dachs, David: *Encyclopaedia Of Pop And Rock* (Scholastic Book Services, 1972)

Stambler, Irwin: *Encyclopaedia of Pop, Rock And Soul* (St Martin's Press, 1974)

Russell, Tony: *The Encyclopaedia Of Rock* (Crescent)

Strong, MC: *The Great Book Discography* (Canongate)

Guitar Player, *Guitar World*, *Total Guitar*, *Rolling Stone* (miscellaneous issues)

Clifford, Mike: *The Harmony Illustrated Encyclopaedia Of Rock* (Harmony Books, 1992)

Pascall, Jeremy: *The Illustrated History Of Rock Music* (Galahad Books)

Obrecht, Jas: *Masters Of Heavy Metal* (Quill, 1984)
Finnis, Rob: *The NME Book Of Rock* (Star Books)

Logan, Nick and Woffinfden, Rob: *The NME Book Of Rock* 2 (Music Sales Limited)

Jacobs, Jack: *Ozzy Osbourne Rock-It Comix* (Rock-It Comix, December 1993)

Ellis, Robert: *The Pictorial Album Of Rock* (Crescent)

Marks, J: *Rock And Other Four Letter Words: Music Of The Electric Generation* (Bantam Books, 1968)

Gillett, Charlie and Frith, Simon: *Rock File 5* (Chartlog, 1967-1977; Panther/Granada)

Fowler, Pete and Annie: *Rock File 5* (Panther/Granada, 1978)

Rees, Dafydd and Crampton, Luke: *Rock Movers And*

Shakers (Billboard Books, 1991)

Elmlark, Walli and Beckley, Timothy Green: *Rock Raps of The '70s* (Drake)

Hounsome, Terry and Chambre, Tim: *Rock Record* (Rock Record, 1979)*

Gross, Michael, Jakubowski, Maxim/Delilah: *The Rock Yearbook 1981* (Grove Press, 1981)

Pareles, Jon and Romanowski, Patricia: *The Rolling Stone Encyclopedia Of Rock 'n' Roll* (ARS Press Book/Summit Books, 1983)

Various: *The Rolling Stone Illustrated History Of Rock 'n' Roll* (*Rolling Stone* Press Book, 1976)**

DeCurtis, Anthony and Henke, James: *The Rolling Stone Illustrated History Of Rock 'n' Roll* (Random House)

Miller, Jim: *The Rolling Stone Illustrated History Of Rock 'n' Roll* (Random House/*Rolling Stone* Press Book)

Editors of Rolling Stone: *The Rolling Stone Record Review* (*Rolling Stone*, 1971)

---

* This tome regaled itself as "the most comprehensive rock reference book compiled to date". Under the Black Sabbath heading, vocalist Osbourne's first name is spelled Ozzie.

* In an article titled "Heavy Metal", the late Lester Bangs wrote, "All heavy metal groups sound alike. Ozzy's vocals sound like Jack Bruce of Cream."

Editors of Rolling Stone: *The Rolling Stone Record Review* (*Rolling Stone*/Pocket Books)

Editors of Rolling Stone: *The Rolling Stone Record Review II* (*Rolling Stone*, 1974)

Editors of Rolling Stone: *The Rolling Stone Record Review II* (*Rolling Stone*/Pocket Books)

Heatley, Michael: *The Ultimate Encyclopaedia Of Rock* (Harper Perennial, 1993)

Waxpaper volume three (Warner Bros in-house publication, 1978)

Bane, Michael: *Who's Who In Rock* (Facts On File)

York, William: *Who's Who In Rock Music* (Scribners)

The Year In Rock (*Billboard* charts/*Musician*, 1981-82)

Marsh, Dave: *For the Record: Black Sabbath – An Oral History* (1998, Avon Books)

Index

The letter n appearing after a page number indicates that the reference is a footnote.